Astrological Guidance
for
Friendship and Profit

Dr. R.N. Vyas

UBSPD
UBS Publishers' Distributors Ltd.
New Delhi Bombay Bangalore Madras
Calcutta Patna Kanpur London

UBS Publishers' Distributors Ltd.
5 Ansari Road, New Delhi-110 002
Bombay Bangalore Madras Calcutta Patna Kanpur London

© R.N. Vyas

First Published 1996

Cover Design : UBS Art Studio

Lasertypeset in 11 pt. Times at Alphabets, New Delhi
and printed atPauls Press, New Delhi

Astrological Guidance
for
Friendship and Profit

To
loving memories of
my eldest brother
Syt. L.V. Vyas

Therefore the love which us doth bind
But Fate so enviously debars
Is the conjunction of the Mind
And opposition of the stars.

Andrew Marvell

CONTENTS

PREFACE

The people whom we encounter during the course of our life can be classified into three categories. The first category consists of those persons whom we appreciate and love; the second category of those persons with whom we try to adjust in one way or the other; and the third category of those persons whom we detest. While developing a friendship or arranging a marriage or entering into a business deal or establishing any personal associations, we shall like to come in contact with the persons of the first category of people as far as possible.

But how to select such people is the problem.

Here astrology can help us a lot. The basic tenet of pragmatism is that what is useful is true. God is true, because faith in God can foster courage and bring happiness in one's life. Voltaire had once stated that if there is no God, we shall have to invent Him. He is so helpful to us. In the same way,

1

astrology is true because it is useful. People from the dim and distant past of humanity to the modern period have conti-nuously reposed faith in astrology and have used it for their purposes.

Moreover, human beings have an innate urge to pry in the future. Astrology is perhaps the only science which can help them in this direction. The present work intends to help a person to find out those persons with whom he can pull on well, whether it is in the domain of marriage or the field of business. The various devices which have been described in the present work shall help a reader to ascertain the persons with whom he can have fruitful relations. Their judicious use is recommended. What is the harm in using them? They shall cost him nothing. On the other hand, they may bring him solace and prosperity.

I shall feel my effort rewarded if the readers are able to derive even a little foresight and satisfaction by using the devices mentioned in this book. I thank the publishers, who enabled me to reach the interested readers through this book. I shall welcome any suggestion from my worthy readers to render the work still more useful to them.

Indore
July 1995
R.N. Vyas

Chapter I

INTRODUCTION

In the present-day world, many modern, educated persons suffer from a duality of nature. They condemn politicians and contend that politics is the 'last resort of a scoundrel'; and, yet, aspire to acquire the highest political positions; they denounce corruption as a moral and social evil, but, at times, tend to indulge in it themselves to gain material advantages. This very dichotomy is evident even in the case of their condemnation of astrology. The somewhat disdainful and supercilious modern-day 'elitist' tries to dismiss astrology as a 'piece of irrational and blind faith', but seeks its shelter whenever he happens to be surrounded by despondency, hardships and difficulties. For example, this author personally knows a professor of a post-graduate institution who used to deride astrology as a 'piece of sheer superstition,' but who rushed to consult many astrologers when he fell ill. His case is a typical one

3

of ambivalence towards astrology, which engulfs the average 'modern' human being.

By nature a human being is extremely inquisitive. He wants to know what the future holds for him. This tendency becomes all the more overpowering when the cloud of misfortune and adversity engulfs him. And as there is no other way of knowing the future, he has to take guidance from astrology. *Jyotisha* (astrology) has been accepted as an important part of the Vedas, and it includes both *ganita* and *phalita*, i.e., the mathematical and predictive portions.

What exactly is astrology? Is it a science? This is a question which has been raised very frequently. The answer is: 'Yes, astrology is a science, because any body of systematized knowledge can be called a science, and astrology is certainly a systematic study of the effects of planets and other celestial bodies on an individual as well as a society'. But astrology is not a material science, such as physics or chemistry, and, therefore, its methods are not based on observation and experiment; on the other hand, its methods are observation and intuition.

Astrology has been used by human beings from time immemorial. If this subject had not been found useful, it would have disappeared long ago. But far from doing so, it is gaining wide popularity day by day. A vast majority of Hindus still consult astrologers before conducting marriage and other ceremonies. Agriculturists and house-builders refer to astrological charts to avoid probable difficulties that may afflict them in course of time. Periodicals all over the world publish daily, weekly, fortnightly or monthly predictions for the benefit of their readers.

In this context, it would be worthwhile to refer to Dr. Hans Eysinik, professor of psychology, General Medicine Hospital, London, who had declared: 'The only conclusion the unbiased observer can come to must be that there do exist a small number of people who obtain knowledge existing in other people's minds or in the outer world by means as yet unknown to science.' The significance of astrology can be inferred from the fact that Michael Gaqueline, professor of statistics and psychology at Sorbonne University, collected one lakh horoscopes and found that a high frequency of births of doctors and a low frequency of births of actors coincided with the position of Mars in the meridian. Similarly, a high frequency of births of doctors with the position of Jupiter in the meridian and a low frequency of births of painters resulted when Jupiter was in the meridian.

In India, astrology has been considered to be a lamp which enables a person to see in the darkness of the future. The present volume has been written with the specific purpose of helping a person in selecting true, reliable friends and trustworthy partners in business. Our social life and also our business life need a guide who could help us in our day-do-day interactions and transactions. Exercising wisdom and precaution in choosing the right persons could avoid the possibility of hardship, despondence or failure that may result later. This book has been written with this clear-cut objective alone. Therefore, the contents deal with only those topics which are considered important from this standpoint.

It would be worthwhile to provide a brief glimpse

of the subsequent chapters. The second Chapter attempts to develop a nexus between astrology and the concept of probability. Also it expounds the main theories of perception. The third Chapter discusses the problems of determinism and human freedom. It is necessary to take up this question before entering the arena of astrology. The fourth chapter shows how astrology is useful even from the standpoint of character analysis, which is supposed to be the field of psychology. The fifth chapter throws light on the nature of astrology. The sixth chapter emphasises the importance of Moon, which occupies a predominant place in the domain of astrology. The seventh chapter describes the nature of *grahas* (planets), which determine people's *rashis*. The eighth chapter seeks to identify the way of determining the factor of friendship (used in a wide sense). The ninth chapter presents the numerological devises for determining friendship, because such devices are found to be more feasible. The tenth chapter cites some instances to amplify the previous chapter. The eleventh chapter is wider in its coverage as it discusses the nature of social relationships. The final chapter (twelfth) presents the birth date guide.

The appendices too have their utility. The first appendix lists the favourable periods of a day for doing any work. The second appendix presents a very easy way of obtaining information on the likely success of an endeavour with the help of a diagram or a number. The subject-matter does not go very deep, but somehow or the other, its utility is universal during the crisis periods. The third appendix is astrologically more important as it depicts the impact of the transit of planets. However, its interpretation requires a knowledge of one's *rashi* or *lagna*. Appendix 4 presents the 'method of pyramids' in order to seek answers to a person's specific questions. In this volume the author's approach to the subject of astro-logy is very practical. The subject-matter aims at helping a reader to seek astrological help for himself without consulting any regular astrologer. Appendix 5 lists the names of important *grahas* and *rashis* and their English equivalents.

Just as an elementary knowledge of medicine may be useful to a person for getting relief without approaching any regular doctor, in the same way, a reading of this book shall equip a reader with that elementary knowledge which may be useful in dealings in regular life.

The readers are, of course, free to use any method shown in this book. However, they should always remember that astrology does not claim any *certainty*. It only claims *probability* i.e., a strong probability, which can be the only worthwhile guide in our human dealings.

Chapter 2

THE CONCEPT OF PROBABILITY AND THE THEORY OF PERCEPTION

In our present-day society, there are certain persons who expect absolute certainty and precision from astrology. They hold the opinion that astrology can be considered a science *only* if it can provide predictions which shall never prove to be false. However, such persons betray their unscientific thinking because modern science itself accepts that certainty cannot be obtained even through elaborate and sophisticated instruments. That is why weather forecasts prove wrong at times.

Science accepts the principle of probability. Even though we may assume that everyone has a rough idea of the meaning of 'probability', we shall try here to elucidate the concept to the extent possible.

Probability stands in between certainty and impossibility. For example, we say that it will probably rain today, or that Mohan shall fail to pass the examination. However, probability in this sense is not a clear concept; it merely indicates a

9

lack of entire conviction that some event will, or will not, happen.

In our ordinary conversation, when we say that 'the occurrence *E* will probably result' we mean that there are stronger reasons for supposing that this occurrence will result than for supposing that it will not. We recognize that an occurrence may be more, or less, probable. There are numerous degrees of probability between the certainty that *E will not happen* and the certainty that *it will happen*. If we want to calculate exactly the probability of the occurrence of event *E*, we must counter the number of reasons that are unfavourable and can, therefore, be offered against the occurrence of *E*.

To count the reasons for and against means to analyse the situation so as to determine what factors are favourable and what are not favourable.

If one tries to analyse a situation without the aid of astrology, one cannot judge the probability so adeptly. But if the help of astrology is sought, the nature of probability can be known in a much better way. It appears that the universe is an organic whole. Hence, planets too are internally, though imperceptibly, connected with individuals. Astrology is able to probe the influence of this interdependence between human beings and planets. No other science except astrology through astrological devices can be helpful in this endeavour.

In this context let us discuss a specific theory of perception advocated by the Nyaya system of Indian philosophy. Ordinarily, perception is defined as 'a cognition due to the stimulation of sense organs by the perceived object'. But some philosophers such as Nyayikas and Vedantins like to define perception in a different manner. The reason advanced is that there are cases where perception is possible even without the aid of sense organs. For instance, if a person sees a snake in a piece of rope, really speaking, there is no snake to stimulate the eyes. Thus, we may state that mental states like pleasure and pain are not perceived through any sense organ. They are directly cognized or perceived by us.

What is common to all types of perception is directness or immediacy of knowledge given by them. For example, when one sees the Sun and the Moon in the sky, one perceives the presence of the Sun directly. Hence, we are said to perceive an object if and when we know it directly, i.e., without taking any help from previous experiences or reasoning process. Hence, Indian thinkers like to define perception as an immediate cognition (*sakshat pratiti*). Nevertheless they still believe that, ordinarily, perception is not possible without sense stimulation by an object.

The Nyaya system has classified perception into two categories, viz. ordinary (*laukika*) and extraordinary (*a-laukika*). In ordinary perception there is the usual sense contact with objects present in front of a person. Such perception is of six kinds: Visual (*chakshusha*); auditory (*shrauta*); tactual (*sparshana*); gustatory (*rasana*); olfactory (*ghranaja*); and the internal (*manasa*) perception.

In extraordinary perception the object is such that it is not ordinarily present and knowledge is conveyed to the mind through an unusual medium. Extraordinary perception is of three kinds. The first is *samanya-lakshana*. For example, when we state 'all men are mortal', we mean that *all men* are mortal, whether they are present in front of us or live in any place not known to us. Here, mortality is attributed to all men without any exception.

But how do we perceive the whole class of men? Of course, no man can perceive the entire class of men. According to the Nyaya system, this entire class can be known only through extraordinary perception, in which the class of men is presented through the class essence or the universal 'manhood'.

An individual can thus state: When I perceive a man, I perceive him as 'man'; otherwise I cannot call him man. Thus all men are perceived by me through this perception of manhood. This perception of the class of men, being due to the perception of the universal (*samanya*) is called *samanya-lakshana* perception, and has been named extraordinary perception as it differs from the ordinary type of perception.

There is a second type of extraordinary perception known as *jnana-lakshana*. We often state when we perceive a piece of ice that it is 'cold'. We also state that 'grass is soft' or 'tea is hot', without actually touching the object. This too is extraordinary perception.

The third kind of extraordinary perception is known as *yogaja pratyakshya*. This perception consists in intuitive perception of all objects, past and future, hidden or seen by a person who has obtained supernatural power due to the practice of yoga. If a person has pursued spiritual practice, extraordinary power is obtained by him.

An astrologer gains intuitive power and knowledge to peep into the world of the future because of leading a spiritual life and through the study of astrological works and of the movement of planets. The horoscope arouses his intuitive power to exert itself. The quality of spiritual life led by an astrologer makes a lot of difference. If a cheat studies astrology and peruses astrological works, his predictions cannot be correct, because predictive ability is not founded on a study of astrological works alone. Such ability requires that one leads a life on a higher plane than that of an average person. Thus an astrologer has a kind of *yogaja* perception, i.e., a power of perception which is borne due to leading a non-fraudulent life as well as due to a study of astrology. If a person leads a pious life, he is able to foresee things even if he has not studied astrology properly. This perpetual power is mystical, if viewed from the standpoint of an ordinary person. But mystery is a part of life. One does not know from where life comes and where does one go after death. An astrologer is thus able to perceive the probability of an event occurring in an efficient manner.

The Bhagavata purana has described the characteristics of Kaliyuga on the basis of this mystical power. Also, it is claimed that Nostradamus (in the sixteenth century) made amazing predictions, which came out to be true subsequently, because of this power. For example, let us note the following prediction about Rajiv Gandhi:

The great Pilot shall be sent for by Royal mandate.
To leave the fleet, and be preferred to a higher place.
Seven years after he shall be countermanded
A barbarian army shall put Venice to fear.

Rajiv Gandhi did play a prominent role in Indian politics right from 1984 to 1991 i.e., for seven years. The word 'Venice' points to Sonia Gandhi, who is an Italian.

Let us consider two more instances from Nostradamus prophecy. The first is concerned with the Indian Revolt (or sepoy Mutiny, as the British term it) of 1857:

News being brought of a great loss,
The report divulged, the camp shall be astonished,
Troops being united and revolted,
The falange shall forsake the great one.

The second prophecy pertains to Napoleon:

An Emperor shall be born in Italy,
Who shall cost the Empire dear.
They shall say, with what peoples he keeps company.
He shall be found less a Prince than a butcher.

Thus we find that it is possible for some people to foresee the coming events. This ability can be called a *yogaja* perception, i.e., a perception which becomes possible through a knowledge of astrology or through intuitive faculty.

Chapter 3

BHAGAVADGITA AND
THE *DAIVA* FACTOR

The *Bhagavadgita* is an important Hindu work. In fact this work is beyond any religious or philosophical creed. It is a work of universal significance and has perennial value.

The *Gita* is famous for its philosophy of *karma yoga*. The *Gita* is the only work that declares that man is 'condemned to be active'. If a person is inactive physically, he may be active mentally. One cannot run away from work. However, it is a mark of philosophic wisdom to work in an intelligent and conscious manner.

The *Gita* presents a logical analysis of action [18th chapter (18-14)]. According to this analysis, every act has five factors (*karanani*), namely,

(1) The basis or seat of action (*adhisthana*).
(2) The agent (*karta*).
(3) Various kinds of methods or instruments (*karanam*).

15

(4) Various types of efforts (*chesta*).

(5) *Daiva* (the Will of God, who rules the universe).

The word *daiva* is sometimes understood in the sense of the accumulated effect of past actions. It is also called fate or destiny. But it will be easier for us to understand it as the will of God. In fact, in our ordinary life we do use the proverb, 'Man proposes but God disposes'. However, there are persons who do not believe in the existence of God. They prefer a term like 'circumstances' as the determining factor. Since we are concerned with the general public, we need not quarrel about semantics. The basic factor is that there is something which is beyond the control of an agent (human being).

It is claimed that Napoleon used to assert: "The term 'impossible' does not exist in my dictionary." The statement is a very brave one on the face of it. But the very fact that his last days were spent in the prison at St. Helena shows that this statement is hollow.

The history of the world reveals that many individuals like Alexander the Great, Changez Khan and Hitler dreamt of conquering the world. They planned and prepared for the attainment of their ambition, but ultimately failed miserably, despite initial successes. Saintly persons like Buddha, Christ, Mohammad and Gandhi, on the other hand, tried to reform the world through their efforts. But despite such efforts, the world has moved in its usual way.

The only inference that can be drawn from these instances is that the world is ruled by God, who cannot be seen through our eyes but can only be experienced like fragrance or light. If man were the maker of history the world would have been much worse because every Alexander would have tried to shape it according to his whims and fancies. One has to become a bit of a philosopher to seek the actual truth.

God has manifested Himself in the forms of the world. Every human being is, therefore, substantially God. However, every being has been endowed with a specific outward personality and has been granted a certain degree of liberty. In the words of the *Gita*, people differ from the standpoints of inner nature and conduct (*guna-karma vibhagashah*). Every individual can play his or her role in the world in a way he or she likes. He or she has enough liberty to think, plan and act. But nobody can interfere with the world order. The world power (God) decides: 'Thus far, and no further'. Hence, a person possesses the liberty to act in a way he or she likes, but does not have the liberty to obtain the result he or she wants to get. Such a person may theoretically assert: 'I can achieve anything', but practically he or she can achieve only as much as does not conflict with the world plan. This world plan extends to every individual and to every atom or particle. This is clear from the statement of Lord Krishna to Arjuna:

Time am I, world-destroying, grown mature, engaged here in subduing the world. Even without the (thy action), all the warriors standing arrayed in the opposing armies shall cease to be. Therefore, arise thou and gain glory. Conquering thy foes, enjoy a prosperous kingdom. By me alone are they slain already. Be thou merely the occasion, O Svayasachina. (XII, 32, 33.)

Let us consider an example to illustrate the foregoing point.

Mohan starts a business. He invests money and labour. He advertises the items which he manufactures. He is definitely free to carry out all these activities. But Mohan cannot command the result. He may incur a loss; or he may be able to earn money. Here 'losing' or 'earning money' falls within the realm of God's plan or will. If Mohan weeps because he has lost money, or rejoices because he has earned money, both acts are rooted in the belief that he can either earn or he may lose. The reality is that Mohan is free only to think, plan and act; i.e., *Karmanye vadhikaraste* (your right exists only up to action). The result rests with *daiva* (the divine will or plan).

There is no doubt that mystery surrounds the *daiva* factor. But through astrology, one can gain a broad vision about it. Nobody can see the future completely, because the divine will is incomprehensible, but it is possible to know it partially.

A Sanskrit *shloka* states:

All the *shastras* (scriptures or sciences) are indirect. They are replete with the contradictory view- points. But astrology is a perceptible and direct *shastra*. The Moon and the Sun bear a standing evidence of this fact.

अप्रत्यक्षाणि शास्त्राणि, विवादस्तेषु केवलम् ।
प्रत्यक्षं ज्योतिषं शास्त्रं चन्द्रार्को यत्र साक्षिणो ।।

The *Gita*, however, does not support the view that a human being is an utterly powerless animal who is incapable of doing anything.

Shri Krishna declared (to Arjuna) who was thinking of leaving the battlefield instead of fighting the Kauravas who were his cousins (brothers) being swayed by the idea: "It would be better for me if the sons of Dhritarashtra, armed with weapons, killed me in battle while I am unarmed and unresisting." Lord Krishna then counselled Arjuna as follows. "Yield not to unmanliness, Arjuna; this attitude is entirely unbecoming of you. Shake off this paltry faint-heartedness, and arise, O oppressor of the foes."

In fact, of the five factors of action described by the *Gita*, viz., *adhishthana, karta, karanam, chesta,* and *daiva*, the first four factors are within the control of a human being. The *daiva* factor is a superpersonal factor. It is the duty of a human being to act to the best of his or her ability. He or she cannot shun activity; but is up to him or her to act vigorously or weakly. If he or she acts efficiently he or she is a winner; if he or she acts inefficiently, he or she is a loser. The reward of an act lies in its efficient execution, and not in its consequence.

The *Gita* declares that one should act in due accordance with one's basic nature. It is degrading to imitate any other person in a blind manner, because all acts are of equal worth, if they are performed in the right spirit.

The *Gita* informs us that human beings can basically be classified into four categories on the grounds of their inner nature (IV, 13). Thus, Brahmin, Kshatriya, Vaishya and Shudra are not the names of classes or castes; they are the names of different states of mentality.

All types of actions have equal merit. Hence, to discard an act that suits one's temperament and rush to imitate others is an act rooted in ignorance of the truth.

The *Gita* is a strong advocate of action. The *daiva*

factor described by the *Gita* has to be understood in the right spirit. To be active does not imply that a human being can attain anything that he or she wants. The universe is ruled by certain principles. Nobody can break them; nobody can take them into his or her own hands.

What one cannot achieve despite one's most sincere and mighty efforts must be attributed to *daiva*. Shakespeare echoes the spirit of the *Gita* in his *Julius Caesar* when he writes:

Why, man, he doth bestride the narrow world
Like a Colossus; and we petty men
Walk under his huge legs, and peep about
To find ourselves dishonourable graves.
Men at some time are masters of their fates;
The fault, dear Brutus, is not in our stars,
But in ourselves, that we are underlings.

Let us elucidate the view of the *Gita* in a different manner. Every person lives in certain environment. All that he or she does, perceptibly or imperceptibly, produces a certain effect in that environment. A human being's body is a very important factor. Without the body no action is possible. Hence, the body may be considered to be the basis of an action. However, the sense of 'I' is needed. This 'I' is the agent. This 'I' is an organic whole of our tendencies. This 'I' is the real person who activates the body and does everything else. But action cannot be performed without any instruments which are assembled by the 'I' to achieve its target. But the mere presence of instruments cannot go very far. A person has to make various attempts to achieve his or her objective. Thus far, every human being is free. But he or she should not forget that there is a factor which makes his or her efforts a success or turns them into a mere failure. This mysterious factor whose presence is experienced by every one of us at times but which cannot be ordinarily explained is called *daiva*.

As a famous poet Omar Khayyam has stated:

The moving finger writes; and having writ
Moves on; nor all thy piety nor wit
Shall lure it back to cancel half a line
Nor all thy tears wash out a word of it.

A student may study day and night, very sincerely. But the objective may not be attained, due to what we call popularly 'bad luck'. God has created every person with a certain objective. If a person, due to negligence, ignorance, egoistic feeling, pride or any other such factor, knowingly or unknowingly, tries to take liberties with the divine plan, he or she is sure to meet with failure.

A person usually fails to foresee the fate of his actions. Hence the best way is to act dexterously and leave the result to God. A human being can neither command success nor can he or she invite failure. Let every sensible person consider victory or failure as the will of God and continue to work in an efficient manner. A successful person is one who acts sincerely and efficiently, and not one who achieves success by chance. Astrology tries to understand the nature of everybody's *daiva* through the study of planets or other such devices. Their efforts merely yield the extent of probability.

Chapter 4

DETERMINISM AND FREEDOM

The most ticklish questions confronting astrology are: "Is everything predetermined? What is the scope of individual freedom?" Before answering these questions, we should make an attempt to understand the concepts of *determinism*, *indeterminism* and *self-determinism*.

Determinism

Determinism implies that everything is predetermined. In other words what is going to happen must happen. Freedom of will is non-existent. In support of this doctrine, the following arguments have been put forth.

Psychological facts

All our volitions are determined by motives and desires. Our will has to obey the commands or motives. When there is a conflict among motives, it is the strongest motive that wins. Will can do nothing in this context. The strength of a motive is determined partly by hereditary factors and partly by environmental factors. Thus every action is bound by previous causes. In support of this view, we presume that human actions are predictable like weather or any other natural phenomenon. If man is truly free, it would be impossible to predict his conduct. Thus, a person who is a congenital cheat is bound to indulge in cheating.

Thus, we may conclude psychological fact indicates that there is no total freedom of will.

Scientific evidence

Science states that there exists a law of causality. Nothing happens without a cause. Freedom of will implies that a person is free to act in any way he likes. This is against the scientific law of causality.

Science also believes in the law of conservation of energy according to which the amount of energy in the universe is constant. Such energy cannot be increased or decreased. This law too cannot accept freedom of will, because it will mean increasing or decreasing the amount of energy. If we accept freedom of will, we shall break this universally accepted law of science.

Science also points out that everything in the universe has evolved out of matter. Charles Darwin accepted this fact. Even the modern theory of evolution, which is known as theory of emergent evolution, holds that even mind has evolved out of matter. It is only a product or epiphenomenon of the brain. As matter has no freedom, the mind too cannot have any freedom.

Theological standpoint

Theology tells us that God has created human beings. He controls their conduct and behaviour. It is, therefore, against the accepted principle of theology to hold the view that man is free. Human freedom shall mean that God is not free and omnipotent.

Determinism, therefore, states that the human will is not free. If this view of determinism is true, then astrology has no utility or significance, because, if whatever is going to happen must happen, then what is the use of knowing the future. Knowlege of the future can have some utility only if man has any power of altering it to a certain extent. When we consider determinism, we find that it has the following weak points:

It is true that motives determine will, but it is forgotten that motives are built by mind itself. An ethical author has stated: "Volition is determined from within the mental principle itself, and not from impulsion from without. It is not external determination by cause, but internal self-determination." External circumstances are many times similar, yet individuals differ in conduct. For example, let us take the example of a family. The children brought up in the same family do not have a similar temperament or identical tendencies. If the external factor alone counts, there should be uniformity in the external behaviour of the members of a family.

It is also not right to deduce determinism on the basis of the fact that sometimes it is possible for us to predict the nature of the conduct of a person. Prediction becomes possible only because a person of free will repeats certain acts out of his own sweet will and such repetition develops a certain character. Prediction is thus an evidence of fixation of character and not an evidence of any deterministic doctrine. Moral life depends on building of certain habits which emerge in the evolution of some specific character. The evidence of science too does not imply determinism. It is true that nothing happens without a cause. Therefore, no act can take place without a cause. But in the case of an act, the self is the cause and not any ulterior entity. Every act manifests the self and contributes towards the formation of character of a specific type.

The law of conservation of energy too does not support determinism. The law merely states that the total amount of energy in the universe remains constant. But it does not claim that the energy remains in the same form. An act of free choice gives a specific form to energy. Energy is not destroyed, it is merely transformed.

The theological argument too fails to support the theory of determinism. If it is accepted that God has created man, then it has to be conceded that man has been granted freedom of will because, in its absence, there shall be no difference between man and a machine or a brute.

Thus, it is clear that the theory of determinism is not correct.

Indeterminism
Some persons have put forward the doctrine of indeterminism, according to which an individual is free to act even against his own character. This

theory even contends that there is a 'free will of indeterminism' lurking in human nature. Because of this free will, a person's acts are free in the sense of being independent of his character too. Explaining this aspect, F.H. Bradley states that: "The self or the will of indeterminism is not the man, not the character at all, but the mere characterless abstraction, which is 'free' because it is indifferent. It has been called 'a will which wills nothing'."

The argument given in support of the doctrine is twofold. When a person acts in a certain way, he has an intuitive feeling that he can act in a contradictory manner too. Similarly, when a person is faced by a temptation, he feels that he can either succumb to the temptation or act against that temptation, i.e., he can resist that temptation. But this view too does not satisfy our reasoning.

The foregoing doctrine merely tells us that an individual can act in a contrary way, if he so likes. But his statement carries a condition. This condition implies that a person could act in another way, if he had developed his character in another way. This means that now the alternative is only theoretical, because his character forces him to act in a specific manner alone.

Let us consider an analogy. Once a creeper has acquired a support, it is not possible to wean away the former from the latter if one does not free it from that support in time. Similarly, one may claim: 'While I am the man I am, it is a manifest absurdity to hold that I can express the opposites in my character.'

The evidence of acting against the resistance too does not support the doctrine. It is not the question of the capacity of acting in an opposite way which is relevant, but is the question of knowing why an individual acts in a specific manner alone. The individual's acting in a specific manner reveals his character.

A.E. Taylor, a well-known philosopher, writes in his *Elements of Metaphysics*: "The real metaphysical objection to indeterminism, however, is not that it is an unprovable and unnecessary hypothesis, but that it involves the denial of rational connection between human actions. By declaring that conduct is not determined by character, it virtually asserts that it is chance which ultimately decides how we shall actually behave in a concrete case. And chance is simply another name for the absence of rational connection."

Self-determinism

The right theory is that the self is the determiner of every action. It chooses every act. That is why we hold a person responsible for his acts. In this connection, we should also keep in mind the Indian theory of *karma*. *Karma* (act) is of three kinds — *sanchita*, *prabdha* and *kriyamana*. Whatever act a person performs, that act leaves behind an effect. Just as when a person sows a seed, and the seed shows its effect in the form of a tree, in the same way, every *karma* leaves behind some effect. Nobody can destroy this rule. The *Rigveda* calls this principle *Rita*. This *Rita* is responsible for the proper functioning of the entire universe. Hence every individual shall have to reap the harvest of his actions. Now the effect of the past acts cannot be experienced at once. Some part of the fruits of an individual's acts is experienced during the present.

This is called *prabdha*, that is, the effects that are being experienced. The rest of the effect shall be experienced in future. This is called *sanchita*, because it is lying in store. But, at the same time, an individual is free to act in the way he likes in his present conduct. This is *kriyamana*, which shall become his destiny in course of time. Thus, whatever is being experienced by a person, pain or pleasure, it is the result of his own acts. And whatever shall be experienced in future, that too, shall be the result of his own acts.

We can now understand why it is necessary that every individual should perform his acts very judiciously. Some persons behave recklessly. They think that nobody is looking at their acts. Hence they indulge in acts that they find to be momentarily pleasant.

Generally it is believed that God keeps the record of each individual's acts in the form of *adrista*. But as God cannot be seen by all, some people think that God is a figment of imagination. He does not exist at all. Hence, one is free to act in any way that one likes. The Mimamsa school, however, has come forward with another theory which does not need the existence of God. According to this theory, every act generates some power. This power is indestructible. If one does something good, good power shall be generated; if one does anything bad, bad power shall be generated. These events happen almost mechanically. There is no escape from them. The result is that the theory of *karma* holds good whether one believes in the existence of God or not.

The *Bhagavadgita* has given a very lucid analysis of *karma*: "There are five factors needed for the accomplishment of all actions," states Lord Krishna. "The seat of action (*adhisthana*), the agent (*karta*), instruments of various sorts (*karanam*), effort (*chesta*) and providence (*daiva*). Whatever action a man undertakes through his body, speech or mind, whether it is right or wrong, these five are its factors" (XVIII, 13, 14, 15).

The *Gita* implies that man is partly free and partly bound: i.e., he is bound by the effect of his past acts (*daiva*).

Just as in a game of cards, a player is bound by the cards he gets, in the same way, one is bound by the effect of one's past acts which is popularly known as 'luck'.

The matter can be understood in another way too. God, or the universe, has a divine plan. Only those acts meet with success which are in tune with that plan.

Astrology unfolds the plan of the destiny of a person. That is, it shows that a person is likely to achieve success or meet with failure as per the stars' positions determined by his past acts. However, astrology tells us only about the possibilities of certain events happening, or not happening.

The reason is obvious. Man is free. He can modify the effects of his acts to certain extent by fresh acts, although everything cannot be changed. The influences of stars merely propel a person; they do not compel him. But because of the lack of such acts as can modify his destiny, man has to suffer the effects of his past acts. Faith in God can do much good, because such a faith implies gaining strength to modify one's destiny. But many persons do not find it possible to develop and sustain such faith.

30

Chapter 5

CHARACTER ANALYSIS AND ASTROLOGY

Many inhabitants of the modern world generally rely on psychology for character analysis and the related vocational guidance. Nowadays, life has become extremely complex. An individual does need some guidance at some stage to ensure the possibility of success and to decrease the quantity of useless effort and expenditure.

Vocational guidance has been accepted as 'the process of helping a person to develop and accept an integrated and adequate picture of himself and of his role in the world of his profession or job; to test this concept against reality; and to connect it with reality, with satisfaction to himself and benefit to society'. This view is shared by eminent persons such as Herbert Sanderson and his associates. The question that now arises is: Is vocational guidance a science or an art? Perhaps, it is both. Guidance is based on factors such as intelligence, special aptitude, personality, physique and academic

31

achievement. Vocational guidance can be extended to cover items such as evaluation at the work place, personality adjustment, marital adjustment, and family relations.

However, the success of vocational guidance based on psychological factors alone is almost impossible to imagine. Factors such as job dissatisfaction, marital maladjustment, social incohesion and disruption in family relations are the factors that reveal that vocational guidance based only on psychology results many times in a great failure.

The situation can be improved if the help of astrology is taken in this connection. Ancient and medieval India relied upon astrology and even, at present, a large number of Indians do consult astrology for solving their problems and they try to obtain the guidance they need.

Astrology goes deeper than psychological guidance. It takes the entire life of an individual, as mirrored in a horoscope, into account. Thus, it has an integrated view of a person. Any study based on such an integrated view is bound to be more correct than that based on a partial view. Astrological rules are not the outcome of mere imagination; they are rules based on the close observation of life. Thus, they are derived from an inductive logical method and possess a great degree of truth. A gifted person can tell more about the personality of an individual through a reading of his horoscope or hand than a board of trained psychological consultants, because the former has an overall, comprehensive view.

From this author's own experience of astrological readings, he can state that a person's inner personality (besides his outer personality) stood revealed the moment his correct horoscope was brought in front of him (the author). Similarly, factors such as the nature of one's life partner, marital adjustment, prospects of earning, and relations with one's relatives became apparent.

Astrology has been found to be so reliable that some gifted Indian doctors used to resort to it for diagnosing the illness of an individual. However, the foregoing remarks should not be interpreted to mean that astrological reading is *always* correct. Just as a sophisticated weapon needs to be efficiently wielded for achieving success, similarly, astrology needs a proper person to grasp correctly its symbolic language. Moreover, in the present age, when even science has discarded the concept of certainty and has wisely accepted the concept of probability, one should be satisfied if one can assess the quantum of probability to the extent possible.

Chapter 6

NATURE OF ASTROLOGY

As already stated, man has an innate tendency of peeping into the future. How otherwise can we account for the rise of what has been called futurology? The publication of books such as *The Devil's Alternative* and *The Third World War* indicates that man would like to know, to the best of his ability, the future events.

Many readers would be astonished to know that the Irish seer, St. Malachy, some 800 years back, was able to draw up a list of the future Popes. He also predicted the events which would take place in Papal history. He had predicted that the Vatican will be destroyed and the papacy will fall in the year 1999. His earlier predictions have so far proved to be correct.

It appears that man possesses not only an intense desire to know the future but he also has some capacity to do so. The future may remain a mystery on the whole. But at least a substantial portion of

35

forthcoming events can be predicted to some extent through astrology. If astrology can know only the probable, its utility would be established, because even modern science does not go beyond it. It is a matter of common experience that many times the weather forecasts based only on scientific technology (however sophisticated) prove inaccurate. Yet, by and large, such forecasts are successful in pointing out the probable weather. Exact knowledge of the future cannot be claimed even by modern science. Hence, it will be futile to expect an exact knowledge of the future in the domain of astrology. Let us concede that having an exact knowledge of the future is a divine attribute and not a human quality. Therefore, one should not measure the worth of astrology merely through the exactness of predictions. The only sensible standard for knowing the future is to understand the nature of the probability of future events. Hence, astrology is merely a science that tries to ascertain such a probability. Even if it fails at times, it remains a science, because other branches of science too cannot claim infallibility.

It is unfortunate that some people try to dismiss astrology as superstition without understanding its objective. Such people are free to have their own opinion, but it is a fact that a great bulk of humanity even now reposes some sort of trust in the potentiality of astrology in obtaining a glimpse of the future.

In India, we find references to astrology even in the ancient scriptures like the *Mahabharata* and the *Ramayana*. Such astrological knowledge was based on astronomical evidence. There appeared an article in *East-West* (in February 1934) which ran as follows: "It '*jyotish*' contains the scientific lore that kept India at the forefront of all ancient nations and made her the Mecca of seekers after knowledge." B. K. Sarkar's work, *Hindu Achievements in Exact Science,* throws enough light on this aspect of ancient astronomical knowledge. Thus, astrological knowledge was the result of astronomical study and not a product of any superstition. The *Bhagavata Purana* contains a narration of Garga (a renowned astrologer). There is a *purana* (named *Bhavishya Purana*) which contains a description of the future of India and the world. The Jataka stories of Buddhism inform us that the birth of Buddha was predicted by astrologers. Apart from ancient India, ancient Greece, Egypt and the Arab nations had developed some kind of a predictive science.

Though it may sound rather odd it is a fact that astrology seems to have become all the more popular in the modern period. A modern nation like the USA, too, has a strong affinity for astrology. Many American periodicals publish weekly, monthly or yearly forecasts, which are quite popular. In modern India too we find the same trend. Even prominent dailies such as *The Times of India* and *The Hindustan Times* publish weekly forecasts. The *Illustrated Weekly of India* had a regular astrological feature. Established weeklies like the *Saptahik Hindustan* and *Dharamyug* used to publish astrological predictions regarding political developments in India.

There is no doubt that astrology is a very useful science and even Dr. Hans Eysenik, professor of psychology, General Medicine Hospital, London, has declared: "The only conclusion the unbiased observer can come to must be that there does exist a small number of people who obtain knowledge existing in other people's minds or in the outer world by means as yet unknown to science."

Astrology is the science which studies the effect and influence of the movements of the planets on the lives of individuals, societies and nations. The influence of the Sun and the Moon, for example, is evident. Other natural phenomena such as the change of the seasons, the rising and ebbing of tides and the eclipses are too obvious to need any detailed description. Astrology, however, should not be confused with fatalism. As a matter of fact, astrology merely describes the nature of events that could emerge in the life of an individual as a result of his own past *karmas*. Moreover, astrology believes that future events can be moulded or modified to some extent through strong efforts. Hence, fatalism is totally ruled out. What is intended is to provide some guidance to an individual so that he can take appropriate steps to reap the full advantage of a coming good opportunity or avoid the malefic effects of an impending bad event by acting more wisely.

Chapter 7

THE MOON AND ITS IMPORTANCE

There was a time, some years ago, when it was believed that astrology was nothing but superstition. But now, intelligent persons have gradually come to have second thoughts and they have accepted the importance of astrology. For example, the well-known psychologist, Carl Jung, wrote to the famous astrologer, B. V. Raman, in his letter of 6 September 1947:

Since you want to know my opinion about astrology, I can tell you that I've been interested in this particular activity of the human mind for more than 30 years. As I am a psychologist, I am chiefly interested in the particular light that the horoscope sheds on certain complications in the character. In cases of difficult psychological diagnosis I usually get a horoscope in order to have a further point of view from an entirely different angle. I must say that I very often found that the astrological data elucidated certain points which I otherwise would have been unable to understand. From such experiences I formed the opinion that astrology is of particular interest to the psychologist, since it contains a sort of psychological experience which we call "projected" — this means that we find the psychological facts as it were in the constellations. This originally gave rise to the idea that these factors derive from the stars, whereas they are merely in a relation of synchronicity with them. I admit that this is a very curious fact which throws a peculiar light on the structure of the human mind.

According to Hindu astrology, the Moon constitutes an important factor in a person's horoscope. The period (*lagna*) during which an individual is born is no doubt very important. This factor throws light on the total personality of an individual. However, it is not possible to know the exact time of birth of every individual. In the absence of such an exact birth time, many horoscopes fail to help us in exact prediction. Under the circumstances, it is better to rely on the *Rashi* based on the movements of the Moon alone. It is the only pragmatic solution to the problem.

According to Indian tradition, the Moon was born from the mind of the Universal Being (*Purusha*). The Moon, therefore, represents the mind. One psychiatrist has stated that the sexual organs are more stimulated on the full Moon day. Every drop of moisture is influenced by the full Moon. The tides are also affected by the full Moon. Menstrual periods too are affected by the full Moon. So much influence is exercised by the Moon on the mind that lovers are called moon-struck. Even in the animal world, both the wild beasts and the domesticated varieties get their mating instincts excited during the full Moon period.

While deciding the question of friendship, therefore, we should look at the *Rashi* (equivalent to the Zodiac sign) determined by the position of the Moon. While a detailed study of an individual's horoscope can definitely give more information about the life of the individual, because horoscopes are not readily available, and friendships cannot be made dependent on the readings of horoscopes, a more handy and easily available means has to be adopted so that some calculations about the future and the nature of friendships can be made at the very outset.

While it is humanly impossible to know exactly in advance the precise course of future events, it is possible to understand the nature of probability on the basis of the readings of *rashis* and their correlation.

Of course, sometimes a person possesses a capacity of knowing the future through intuition. His intuition gets aroused through the nature of interrelationship that takes place between two or more *rashis*. However, we should know more about the of nature *rashis* before we proceed further.

There are twelve *rashis* viz., Mesha, Vrishabha, Mithuna, Karka, Simha, Kanya, Tula, Vrishchika, Dhanu, Makara, Kumbha, and Meena. There are nine *grahas* (planets) recognized by Indian astrology, viz., Surya (the Sun), Chandra (the Moon), Brihaspati (Jupiter), Mangala (Mars), Shukra (Venus), Budha (Mercury), Shani (Saturn), Rahu and Ketu. Of these nine *grahas* the first seven are fundamental ones. The remaining two are merely shadowy in nature.

Surya represents the *atma* (soul) of the Universal Being; Chandra the mind; Mangala the prowess; Budha the speech; Guru knowledge (*jnana*) and happiness (*sukha*); Shukra the sexual urge (*kama*); and Shani unhappiness.

Surya and Chandra are kings: Mangala is the commander-in-chief; Budha is prince; Guru and Shukra are ministers; and Shani is the servant.

The colours of the *grahas* are as follows:

Surya	*Taamra* (copper-like)
Chandra	*Shubhra* (white)
Mangala	*Rakta* (red)
Budha	*Harita* (green)
Brihaspati	*Pita* (yellow)
Shukra	*Chitra* (variegated)
Shani	*Krishna* (black)

The gods of the various *grahas* are as follows:

Surya	Agni
Chandra	Jala
Mangala	Kartikeya
Budha	Hari
Brihaspati	Indra
Shukra	Indrani
Shani	Brahma

42

The various *grahas* have been associated with the different *varnas*:

- Shukra and Brihaspati (Guru) are the lords of Brahmana *Varna*.
- Mangala and Surya are the lords of Kshatriya *Varna*.
- Chandra is the lord of Vaishya *Varna*.
- Budha is the lord of Shudra *Varna*.
- Shani is the lord of the untouchable class.
- Rahu is the lord of the non-community (*mlechchha*)

The different tendencies of the *grahas* are as follows:

- Chandra, Surya and Brihaspati (Guru) are the possessors of *satva guna*, i.e., an ideal and pious character.
- Budha and Shukra are the possessors of *Rajas* quality, i.e., they are worldly and material in character.
- Mangala and Shani possess *Tamas*; i.e., are idle, lazy, and inert by nature.

Chapter 8

THE NATURE OF *GRAHAS* AND *RASHIS*

Surya has been depicted as possessing a square body. His skin carries a lustre and his eyes are yellow. His nature is affected by *pitta* (bile). There are very few hairs on his head. His bones are strong. His colour is a combination of red and black. His eyeballs contain some brownness and redness. His arms are long. He dons a red dress. By nature Surya is courageous and formidable. The Sanskrit version is as follows:

Pittāsthisāró lpakacaścaraktaśyāmakŗtih syānmadhupingalāksah kausumbhāvāśascatura sradehah śūrah pracandah prthubāh urarkah

Chandra is visualized as round. He has *vata* (wind) and *kapha* (phlegm). His eyes are beautiful. His body is white. The hairs on his head are small and black. His body contains a lot of blood. His speech is sweet. He wears a white dress. Bodily and mentally, he is delicate. He is learned:

Sthulo yuva ca sthavirah krśah sitah kāntekśanascasitasùksma murdhajah
raktaikasāro mrduvāk sitānsuko gaurah saśi vātakaphātmako mrduh.

Mangala's appearance is cruel. He is young. He has *pitta*. He is fickle by nature. His waist is thin. The hairs on his head are curly and bright. By nature, he is ferocious. His body is red and he puts on red clothes. He is very noble by temperament:

Madhye krśah kuncitadiptakeśah krurekśanah paittikau graphih raktāmbarraktatanurmahijascandó tyudāra starunó timajjah.

Budha has *vata*, *kapha*, and *pitta*. He is fond of laughter and his spoken words contain many shades of meaning. The lustre of his body is like a leaf of new grass. He is full of nerves. By nature he speaks sweetly. He is well shaped. He is jolly. He has skin as a dominant factor. His eyes are large. He puts on green clothes:

Dūrvālatāsyāmatanustridhātumiśrah sirāvānma dhuroktiyuktah raktāyatākśo haritānśukastvaksāro budho hāsyarucih samangah

Guru's body is huge. He possesses *kapha*. The colour of both his hair and eyes is yellow. His chest is strong. He is very wise. His voice is loud like a lion's. He is moneyed but fat:

Pitadyutih pingakacekśanah syāt pīnonnatorāsca brhaccharirāh kaphatmkah śresthamatih suredyah simhābjanadasća vasupradhānah

Sukra possesses a beautiful body and eyes. He has curly black hair. He is always happy. He dons clothes of many hues. *Kapha* and *vata* are dominant in him.

His colour is white:

*Citrāmbarākuncitakrsnakesah sthùlāngadehaśca kaphānilātmā
durnvānkurābhah   kamano   viśālanetro   brguh
sādhitaśuklavrddhih.*

Shani has a long physique. His hair is hard. He is very lazy and docile. His eyes are deep and he looks downward. He is weak and full of nerves. He is black in colour. *Vata* is dominant in him. Temperamentally, he is cruel and is a backbiter. He is foolish. His teeth and nails are large. His limbs are hard. He is impure. He is ferocious in appearance and, by nature, he is short-tempered. He puts on black clothes. He has an elderly appearance. *Tamas* qualities are dominant in him:

*Pangurnimnavilocanah krśatanurdīrghah sirāló 'lasah
krsnāngah pavanātmako' tipiśunah snāyvātmako nirghranah
mūrkhah sthūlanakhadvijah parusaromangó' śucistamaso
raudrah krodhaparo jarāparinatah krsnāmbaro bhaskarih.*

The foregoing descriptions of *grahas* are merely symbolic. These descriptions suggest that persons in whose horoscopes these *grahas* are dominant possess the related qualities. Also, those persons whose *rashis* have these *grahas* as lords possess these specific marks. We can summarize these descriptions in the following chart:

Names of the graha	Physical quality	Mental quality
Surya	Strong bones; hair on head scanty; square shape of body; long arms; brown eyes. *Pitta* dominant.	Self-confidence; assertive; and couragen
Chandra	but weak body; small but black hair; beautiful eyes; body contains a lot of blood; white complexion; big build; young appearance. Complaints of *kapha* and *vata*.	Delicate nature; easily ruffled; sweet speech; likes white clothes and white coloured objects.
Mangala	Reddish body; small waist; curly hair; piercing eyes. Complaints of *pitta*.	Hot temperament; fond of red objects and clothes; fierce but noble.
Budha	Good skin texture; full of nerves; big eyes; well-shaped body. Complaints of *vata*, *kapha*, and *pitta*.	Jolly; sweet tongued; capacity for adjustment.
Guru	Pale colour of physique; big body; eyes and hair somewhat brown; moneyed. complaints of *kapha*.	Pious and intelligent.
Shukra	Black and curly hair; white complexion; beautiful appearance; big eyes. *Pitta* dominant.	Sexual desire dominant; sense of beauty developed.
Shani	Deep-seated eyes; tall but thin body; nerves noticeable on the body; big teeth and nails; elderly appearance. *Vata* dominant.	Indolent and somewhat cruel nature; ascetic.
Rahu	Big build.	Non-religious; deceptive.
Ketu	Red eyes; tall build.	Hard tone of speech

Key words suggesting a person's nature

Herein below are stated certain key words or terms suggesting the basic nature of affinity for persons under the influence of the following individual planets:

Surya (Sun)

Authoritativeness; spirit of commanding; conceit; confidence; eminence; ability to govern; influential traits; spirit of leadership; management capacity; love for prestige; tendency to attain renown; love for being in the spotlight; and strong willpower.

Chandra (Moon)

Changeable character tendencies; emotionality; love for items such as brooks, gardens and fountains; impressionableness; tendency to moods; sentimentalism; love for pearls and white objects; tendency to be deeply attached to wife or women; love for popularity; attachment to maternal relations; love for mother; and homesickness.

Budha (Mercury)

Accountancy; agency; advisory capacity; advertisement auditorship; dealership in, or attachment to, books; broadcasting; column writing; commentary giving; communication; correspondence; editorship; journalism; lecturing; oratory; publication; psychiatry; research; typing; business; talkativeness; wittiness; writing; salesmanship; and interviewing; short journeys; libraries; and periodicals.

Shukra (Venus)

Art; adornment; attachment; amusement; attractiveness; beauty; charm; clothes; celebrations; comforts; cosmetics; courtesy; courtship; culture; decorations; diplomacy; elegance; enjoyment; entertainment; fun;

friendship; gentility; glamour; hospitability; jewellery; luxury; good manners; ornaments; parties and popularity; romance; sex appeal; tactfulness; and woman.

Mangala (Mars)

Adventure; aggression; anger; belligerence; boldness; bravery; combat; courage; cruelty; defiance; energy; exercise (physical); impatience; impulsiveness; initiative; masculinity; rashness; rebelliousness; ruggedness; competitive sports; stamina; strength; virility; fearlessness; and undaunted efforts.

Guru (Jupiter)

Affluence; benediction; philosophical, religious and legal books; religious ceremonies; temples and other religious shrines; charity; education; corpulence; legal counselling; law courts; foreign countries; devotion; ethical life; faith; generosity; honesty; long journeys; humour; literature; philosophy; profession of physician; priesthood; prosperity; religion; sermons; sincerity; worship; scripture; and happiness.

Shani (Saturn)

Ageing; afflictions; austerity; bereavement; caution; conscientiousness; conservative attitude; depression; despair; discipline; doubting; economical; frugal; frustrated; hardship; hermit like tendency; humility; inertia; sense of inferiority; loneliness; meditation; perseverance; prudent; quiet; regularity; responsibility; sceptic attitude; stoic attitude; love for traditions; and worry.

Rahu

Charlatans; cheats; conspiracy; deceit; double dealing; intrigue; and treachery;

Ketu

Underworld; humanitarian; and unconventional.

Rahu and *Ketu* are supposed to be shadow planets. They are considered to exert influences similar to Saturn and Mars. To some extent, the aforementioned key words are merely suggestive. It should be noted that a reading of a horoscope requires an assimilation of the tendencies suggested by different planets in a systematic manner. Hence, reading of a horoscope requires a logical faculty as well as a great deal of experience and proficiency. Further, interpretation of a horoscope requires a highly developed intuitive faculty too. Hence a real astrologer's job is more complex than that of a simple scientist.

Characteristics of *rashis*

Much like the *grahas*, the different rashis too possess distinctive characteristics, which help us in understanding the natures of persons governed by the specific *rashis*.

	राशी	चरणासर								
1.	मेष	यू,	ये,	यो,	ला,	ली,	लू,	ले,	लो,	अ
2.	ऋषभ	ई,	उ,	ए,	मे,	वा,	वी,	वू,	वे,	वो
3.	मिथुन	का,	की,	कू,	ध,	ड,	छ,	के,	को,	हा
4.	कर्क	ही,	हू,	हे,	हो,	डा,	डी,	डू,	डे,	डो
5.	सिंह	मा,	मी,	मू,	मे,	मो,	टा,	टी,	टू,	टे
6.	कन्या	टो,	पा,	पी,	पू,	य,	ण,	ठ,	पे,	पा
7.	तुला	रा,	री,	रु,	रे,	रो,	ता,	ती,	तू,	ते
8.	वश्रिक	तो,	ना,	नी,	नू,	ने,	नो,	या,	यी,	यू
9.	धनु	ये,	यो,	भा,	भी,	भू,	धा,	फा,	ढा,	भे
10.	मकर	भो,	जा,	जी,	खी,	खू,	खे,	खो,	गा,	गी
11.	कुम्भ	गू,	गे,	गो,	सा,	सी,	सू,	से,	सो,	दा
12.	मीन	दी,	दू,	थ,	क,	स,	दे,	दो,	था,	थी,

(जू, जे, जो, श्र (मकर राशी)

51

The determination of a *rashi* is based on the first letter of an individual's name. There are twelve *rashis* as now tabulated.

	Name of the rashi	First letter							
1.	Mesha	cū,	ce,	co,	lā,	lī,	lū,	le,	lo,	a
2.	Vrishabha	ī,	u,	ai,	o,	vi,	vū,	ve,	vo	
3.	Mithuna	ka,	ki,	ku,	gha,	kr,	cha,	ke,	ko,	ha
4.	Karka	hī,	hū,	he,	ho,	dā,	dī,	dū,	de,	do
5.	Simha	mā,	mī,	mū,	me,	mo,	tā,	ti,	tū,	te
6.	Kanya	to,	pa,	pī,	pū,	sa,	na,	dha,	pe,	po
7.	Tula	rā,	ri,	ru,	re,	ro,	tā,	ti,	tū,	te
8.	Vrishchika	to,	nā,	nī,	nū,	ne,	no,	yā,	yī,	yu
9.	Dhanu	ye,	yo,	bhā,	bhū,	bhī,	dhā,	phā,	dhā,	bhe,
10.	Makara	bho,	jā,	jī,	khī,	khū,	khe,	kho,	gā,	gī
11.	Kumbha	gū,	ge,	go,	sā,	sī,	su,	se,	so,	dā
12.	Meena	dī,	du,	tha,	jha,	de,	do,	ca,	cā,	cī.

We now tabulate the individual *grahas* governing different *rashis*.

Name of the *rashis*	Graha
Mesha and Vrishchika	Mangala
Vrishaba and Tula	Shukra
Mithuna and Kanya	Budha
Karka	Chandra
Simha	Surya
Dhanu and Meena	Guru
Makara and Kumbha	Shani

Characteristic features of individual *rashis*
Mesha:

The person governed by this *rashi* possesses a fair amount of independent nature. He has an independent mind. He does not follow the conventions slavishly. He tries to be scientific and penetrating in his thinking, and makes great efforts in the field of education. He is easily excitable, but cools down quickly. He is obstinate, outspoken and free from timidity. He likes to indulge in talking but is rather lazy to do things practically. He is likely to suffer from diseases caused by heat and also from piles. He is not stout, and his features are likely to be good. He is afraid of water. He is fond of travelling. He is likely to be sensuous. His digestion is not very strong.

Vrishabha:

A person governed by this sign is not tall and thin. His face is big and his thighs are large. His tendencies are like those of a bull. That is, he may attack a stranger, if provoked. He follows his own principles. His memory is likely to be sharp. His physical and mental capacity is strong. He possesses a superiority complex. He is likely to be fond of physical beauty and may be extremely passionate. He is likely to succeed as an author. He pursues his chosen path steadfastly. When provoked, he is likely to become extremely angry. He is likely to be practical in his life. He is likely to suffer from sexual diseases or nervous complaints. If one divides his life into three parts, one can say that the second and third parts of his life are likely to be much better than the first one.

Mithuna:

A person governed by this *rashi* is likely to be tall and may possess a snubbed nose and a big forehead. He has a wavering mind and a nervous temperament. He is fond of talking or writing or reading. He possesses a liking for various things and knows something about almost everything. He is likely to be quite intelligent and has a capacity of knowing future events rather intuitively. He cannot forget wrong acts that he had committed, and, therefore, he may harbour a sense of guilt. He is likely to be greatly influenced by his environment. He is not fond of travelling and prefers to stay at home. He is likely to shine as a journalist.

Karka:

A person ruled by this *rashi* is wise and is fond of journeys by boat or ship. He walks swiftly. He is talkative, he is frugal but laborious. He is deeply attached to his family. He is sensitive and nervous. He has a large number of business plans. He is self-dependent and possesses integrity. He loves justice and fairplay. He has a medium stature and obeys women rather readily.

Simha:

A person who is governed by the Simha *rashi* has an impressive appearance. He is bold and courageous. He is ambitious. He possesses a steady intelligence. He has a philosophical tendency and is fond of reading. He may possess egoistic traits and has a tendency of flying into a rage at the slightest provocation. He rarely tolerates opposition and loves to dominate others.

Kanya:

A person born under this *rashi* is worldly wise and intelligent. He can be a good author or a journalist. He has a sweet manner of speaking and can befriend people easily. He knows the secret of adjustment.

He may be fond of music and fine arts, too, at times. But he is also likely to be nervous by temperament and may lack courage. He is of medium sized, and may take advantage of other's property and money, if he gets a chance.

Tula:
A person ruled by this sign has a good personality. He is sensual by temperament. He has the capacity of weighing both sides of an issue and possesses foresight. He is firm in his convictions. He is an idealist by temperament, and has little practical acumen. He can exert influence over others in a subtle way. He relies on his power of intuition. He is so very honest that he does not make any compromise on fundamental principles and is prepared to make any sacrifice to uphold his values.

Vrishchika:
A person ruled by this sign is an unstable lover and seeks excitement. He preaches that one should abstain from sensual things but he himself is attached to them. He does not accept conventions and traditions easily. He may be a good conversationalist, but would not make many friends because of his independent nature. He can be a good administrative officer.

Dhanu:
A person governed by this planetary sign is usually fat. He prefers to follow conventions and traditions. He is interested in occult sciences. He is religious and God-fearing to a certain extent. He is fond of food. He is pure at heart and is always busy in

doing something or the other. He is courageous and generally overcomes his opponents. He is generally moneyed and has access to highly placed persons.

Makara:

A person ruled by this sign is very ambitious, but, by temperament he is lazy. He is modest and liberal. He can be stoical to an extent. He is normally accommodative, but can be short-tempered at times. He is a whimsical person. He sympathizes with persons affected by adversity and has compassion for the down-trodden.

Kumbha:

A person born under the influence of this *rashi* is intelligent and warm-hearted. However, he can become angry at the slightest provocation, but calms down within no time. He is helpful by nature. He can be a good thinker and a successful author. He is shy and does not like to exhibit his talent to everybody. He has great powers of intuition and can judge others in a remarkable manner. His fortunes are not steady. He can be a profound philosopher, if he so chooses. He is normally tall.

Meena:

A person born under the influence of this sign has proportionate limbs. He has a handsome body. His eyes are beautiful. He is a person who never shows any ungratefulness. He is fond of learning and is satisfied with his wife. He is likely to be reserved by nature. Moreover, he is likely to be orthodox. He is not a spendthrift. He tries to adjust with everybody and sometimes lacks self-confidence.

We may summarize the indications of every *rashi* in the following manner.

Mesha *rashi* stands for energy, activity, effort and audacity. It is indicative of self-confidence, frankness, bluntness, boldness, impulsiveness, physical vitality, an irascible temperament, a spirit of independence and strength.

Vrishabha *rashi* depicts a fondness or affinity for music, beauty, artistic environment, pleasure. Such a person dislikes change. This *rashi* indicates a tendency to fly into a great rage, if provoked. Strong prejudices, rigid attitudes, and fixed opinions are also indicated.

Mithuna *rashi* indicates a restlessness expressing itself in the manner of walking quickly and in rapid movement of hands while talking. Versatility is the hallmark of this sign. Fluency in speech and writing and a love for variety are the other noticeable traits.

Karka *rashi* indicates the qualities of sensitivity, and attachment to one's home. Fluctuating mind, sympathy for sufferers, capacity for adapting to every situation and live moral conviction are other characteristics of this *rashi.*

Simha *rashi* represents characteristics such as a dignified personal appearance, an ability to impress and lead others, administrative capacity, a dashing nature, an ostentatious spirit and a confident and egoistic temperament.

Kanya *rashi* stands for a quiet, reserved and methodical, but practical, temperament. Traits such as a tendency to analyse a situation carefully, tactfulness and diplomatic observation and ability to take action are dominant.

Tula *rashi* indicates a sense of balance; i.e., there is a balance between thinking and planning. The presence of a strong sense of justice and the absence of favouritism are prominent features. A balance between thought and emotion equips Tula *rashi* with the requirements of a happy life. This *rashi* opens up a wide field of friendship. Other people's affection is won rather readily.

Vrishchika *rashi* stands for determination and courage, strong likes and dislikes, extremes of love and hate. A person born under this *rashi* can overcome any obstacle that may come in his way as a result of his determined will and zeal.

Dhanu *rashi* indicates a desire and a will to be free, a sense of over-confidence, honesty, generosity and interest in spiritual matters. A person born under this *rashi* does not beat about the bush and comes straight to the point in an undisguised manner.

Makara *rashi* indicates self-control and strong will. A person born under this *rashi* is quite practical and thrifty. Ambition, love of power and an ability to execute plans effectively are present in an ample measure in a person belonging to this *rashi.*

Kumbha *rashi* indicates a genial person having a sense of dedication and sincerity. A person belonging to this *rashi* is broadminded and completely humane. He can befriend any person within no time and tries to maintain this relationship as long as possible. Such a person holds strong opinions and cannot be swayed by any argument easily. He is quite logical and rational in his approach. He is patient and tolerant and is very dependable.

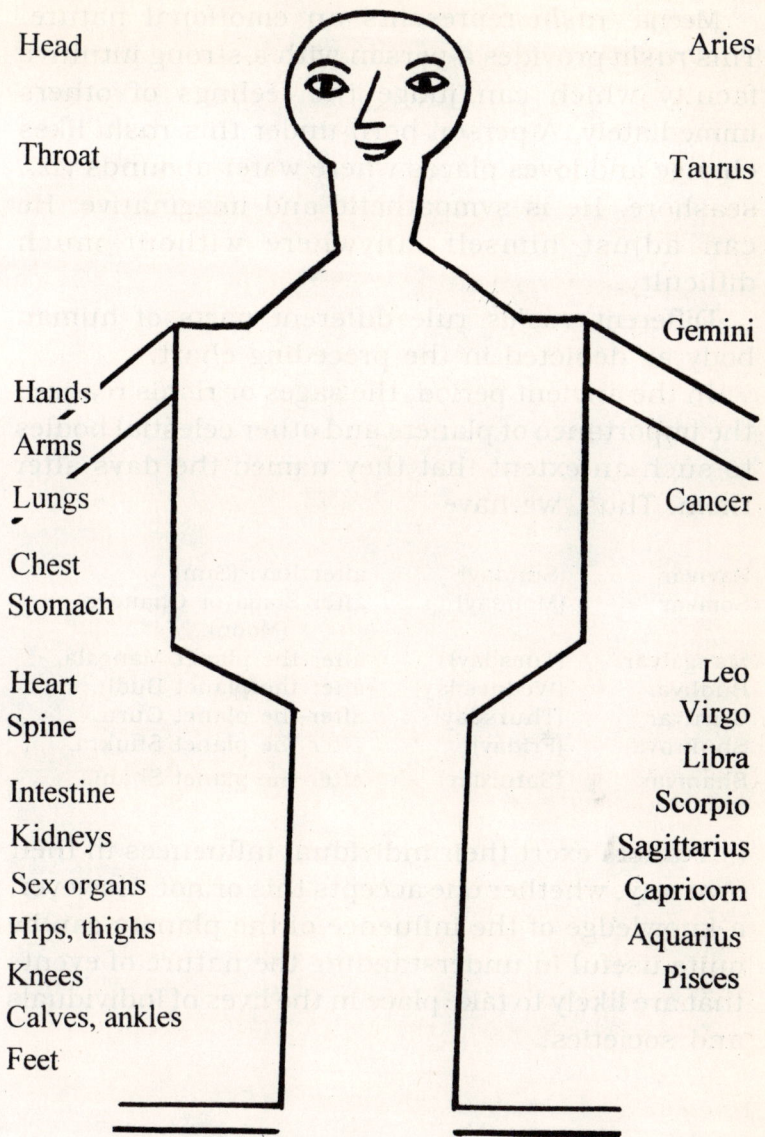

Head — Aries

Throat — Taurus

Gemini

Hands

Arms

Lungs — Cancer

Chest
Stomach

Heart — Leo

Spine — Virgo

Libra

Intestine — Scorpio

Kidneys — Sagittarius

Sex organs — Capricorn

Hips, thighs — Aquarius

Knees — Pisces

Calves, ankles

Feet

Meena *rashi* represents an emotional nature. This *rashi* provides a person with a strong intuitive faculty which can judge the feelings of others immediately. A person born under this *rashi* likes change and loves places where water abounds viz., seashore. He is sympathetic and imaginative. He can adjust himself, anywhere without much difficulty.

Different *rashis* rule different parts of human body as depicted in the preceding chart.

In the ancient period, the sages or rishis realized the importance of planets and other celestial bodies to such an extent that they named the days after them. Thus, we have

Ravivar	(Sunday)	after Ravi (Sun).
Somvar	(Monday)	after Soma or Chandra (Moon).
Mangalvar	(Tuesday)	after the planet Mangala.
Budhvar	(Wednesday)	after the planet Budh.
Guruvar	(Thursday)	after the planet Guru.
Shukravar	(Friday)	after the planet Shukra.
Shanivar	(Saturday)	after the planet Shani.

Planets exert their individual influences in their own way, whether one accepts this or not. However, a knowledge of the influence of the planets can be quite useful in understanding the nature of events that are likely to take place in the lives of individuals and societies.

Chapter 9

HOW TO DETERMINE LIKELY FRIENDSHIP

It is not the object of this book to present any systematic and lengthy account of astrology. Its only objective is to highlight certain astrological devices which may be used by a lay reader for identifying those persons who are likely to establish and sustain good relations with him in case he wants to have any dealing with them. Such precautions may help him in avoiding any future legal controversies and disappointments. We have already discussed in the last chapter how a *rashi* has to be determined. Now we can proceed further to find how the different types of relations among various *rashis* and *grahas* can be determined.

The following chart presents details of planetary friendship.

Grahas	Friends	Neutrals	Enemies
Sun (Simha)	Moon, Mars, Jupiter (Karka, Mesha, Vrishchika, Dhanu and Meena)	Mercury (Mithuna and Kanya)	Saturn and Venus (Makara, Kumbha, Vrishabha and Tula)
Moon (Karka)	Sun and Mercury (Simha, Mithuna and Kanya)	Mars, Jupiter, Saturn and Venus (Mesha, Vrishchika, Dhanu, Meena, Makara, Kumbha, Vrishabha and Tula)	None
Mars (Mesha and Vrishchika)	Jupiter, Moon, and Sun (Dhanu, Meena, Karka, and Simha)	Saturn and Venus (Makara, Kumbha, Vrishabha and Tula)	Mercury (Mithuna and Kanya)
Mercury (Mithuna and Kanya)	Sun and Venus (Simha, Vrishabha and Tula)	Saturn, Mars and Jupiter (Makara, Kumbha, Mesha, Vrishchika, Dhanu and Meena)	Moon (Karka)
Jupiter (Dhanu and Meena)	Sun, Moon and Mars (Simha, Karka, Mesha and Vrishchika)	Saturn (Makara and Kumbha)	Mercury and Venus (Mithuna, Kanya, Vrishabha and Tula)
Venus (Vrishabha and Tula)	Mercury and Saturn (Mithuna, Kanya, Makara and Kumbha)	Mars and Jupiter (Mesha, Vrishchika, Dhanu and Meena)	Moon and Sun (Karka and Simha)
Saturn (Makara and Kumbha)	Venus and Mercury (Vrishabha, Tula, Mithuna and Kanya)	Jupiter (Dhanu and Meena)	Mars, Moon and Sun (Mesha, Vrishchika, Karka and Simha)

The foregoing chart makes this point evident that if a person is governed by a *rashi* mentioned in the first part, he shall have good relations with persons whose *rashis* are mentioned in the second part. He shall not have very bad relations with the persons whose *rashis* are mentioned in the third part. Finally, he cannot have congenial relations with the persons whose *rashis* are mentioned in the third part.

The chart only provides a general indication. We can also ascertain a still closer relationship. For this purpose, we must find out the relationships for temporary friendship, tabulated as follows:

Rashi	Rashi(s) for temporary friendship
Mesha	Vrishabha, Mithuna, Karka, Makara Kumbha and Meena
Vrishabha	Mithuna, Karka, Simha, Kumbha, Meena and Mesha
Mithuna	Karka, Simha, Kanya, Meena, Mesha and Vrishabha
Karka	Simha, Kanya, Tula, Mesha, Vrishabha and Mithuna
Simha	Kanya, Tula and Vrishchika
Kanya	Tula, Vrishchika, Dhanu, Mithuna, Karka and Simha
Tula	Vrishchika, Dhanu, Makara, Karka, Simha and Kanya
Vrishchika	Dhanu, Makara, Kumbha, Simha, Kanya and Tula
Dhanu	Makara, Kumbha, Meena, Kanya, Tula and Vrishchika
Makara	Kumbha, Meena, Mesha, Tula, Vrishchika and Dhanu
Kumbha	Meena, Mesha, Vrishabha, Vrishchika, Dhanu and Makara
Meena	Mesha, Vrishabha, Mithuna, Dhanu, Makara and Kumbha

Excellent relationships can be determined by finding a combination of permanent friendship and temporary friendship; the details are tabulated as follows:

Rashi	*Rashi(s)* of best friend
Mesha	Dhanu and Meena
Vrishabha	Mithuna and Kumbha
Mithuna	Simha and Vrishabha
Karka	Simha, Kanya and Mithuna
Simha	Karka
Tula	Kanya
Vrishchika	Dhanu and Simha
Dhanu	Vrishchika
Makara	Kumbha and Tula
Kumbha	Meena and Dhanu
Meena	Mesha

Besides the foregoing, the following relationships between *rashis* also prove remarkably beneficial.

Rashi	Beneficial *rashis*
Mesha	Simha and Dhanu
Vrishabha	Kanya and Makara
Mithuna	Tula and Kumbha
Karka	Vrishchika and Meena
Simha	Dhanu and Mesha
Kanya	Makara and Vrishabha
Tula	Kumbha and Mithuna
Vrishchika	Meena and Karka
Dhanu	Mesha and Simha
Makara	Vrishabha and Kanya
Kumbha	Mithuna and Tula
Meena	Karka and Vrishchika

The following table provides a way by which *animosity* existing between different *rashis* may be determined.

Initial letters of a person's name	Hostile *rashis* to be determined by the initial letters of the name
1. Sa, Sa, Sa, Ha	Ta, Tha, Da, Dha, Ha
2. Ya, Ra, La, Va	Ca, Cha, Ja, Jha, Ña
3. Pa,Pha,Ba, Bha, Ma	Ka, Kha, Ga, Gha, Ña
4. Ta, Tha, Da, Dha, Ña	A, I, U, E, O
5. Ta, Tha, Da, Dha, Ña	Sa, Sa, Sa, Ha
6. Ca, Cha, Ja, Jha, Ña	Ya, Ra, La, Va
7. Ka, Kha, Ga, Gha, Ña	Pa, Pha, Ba, Bha, Ma
8. A, I, U, E, O	Ta, Tha, Da, Dha, Na

Let us consider a specific example. A person named Ramachandra or Rustam or Raymond shall not have friendly relations with Chandrashekhar, Chand Khan or Charles.

It should be noted that the different devices should not be confused with each other. A person should adopt only one of the aforementioned devices at one time.

Chapter 10

THE NUMEROLOGICAL DEVICE

Apart from the devices mentioned in the previous chapter, there is another device through which the possibility existing for developing friendship or good relations can be determined. Probably this is a more convenient device. Of course, one should not think that any device can give the exact truth. Only probabilities can be determined. We shall concentrate here on the name alone, because it is invariably difficult to obtain the birth dates of persons. Sometimes due to ignorance, some people just do not know their birthdates, sometimes, they are reluctant to divulge them. Moreover, it appears rather odd to enquire about anybody's birth date unless one has an intimate relationship with that person.

In cases where the full name is known, the number value of the full name should be determined; in cases where only the initials and surnames are known, their number value should be calculated. But if an individual takes the full name of a person with whom he wants to deal with, that individual should also take his own full name into consideration. If the initials of the person are taken into consideration then one's own initials, too, should be considered. In other words, there should be uniformity in calculation.

We now provide (in a tabular form) the number values of various English letters:

A—1	F—8	K—2	P—8	U—6	Z—7
B—2	G—3	L—3	Q—1	V—6	
C—3	H—5	M—4	R—2,9	W—6	
D—4	I—1,9	N—5	S—3	X—5	
E—5	J—1	O—7	T—4	Y—1	

The foregoing number values can be stated in another way so that they can be remembered rather easily:

1	A,I,J,Q,Y	Sometimes the following number is also accepted:
2	B, K, R	
3	C, G, L, S	
4	D, M, T	
5	E, H, N, X	9 I R
6	U, V, W	
7	O, Z	
8	F, P	

The discerning reader must have understood by now that the total letter value of the letters of a person's name has to be calculated by adding the value of every letter of a name. After the addition has been done, the result is to be put in the form of any numeral from 1 to 9, thus 11 becomes 2, 19 becomes 1(9+1=10; 1+0=1) , 26 becomes 8, 25 becomes 7 and so on and so forth.

The friendly figures have to be found out with the help of the following chart:

Root number	Friendly number	The most friendly number
1	5	2,7
2	6,3,8	5
3	8	2,7,9
4	5	2,7
5	3	1,4
6	3	-
7	6,3,8	5
8	3	-
9	8	-

The following numbers correspond to the *rashi* mentioned in the second column.

Number	*Rashi(s)*
1	Simha
2	Karka
3	Dhanu
4	Kumbha
5	Mithuna and Kanya
6	Vrishabha and Tula
7	Meena
8	Makara
9	Mesha and Vrishchika

The following numbers have the respective auspicious days:

Number	Day (s)
1	Sunday,Wednesday,Thursday
2	Monday,Tuesday,Friday
3, 7	Thursday,Sunday,Tuesday
8	Saturday,Thursday
5	Wednesday,Sunday,Saturday
6	Friday,Monday,Tuesday
9	Tuesday,Monday,Thursday,Friday
4	Monday,Tuesday,Friday
7	Sunday,Monday,Wednesday,Thursday.

The following numbers shall be found favourable on the dates given in the second column.

Number	Dates
1	1,3,5,7,10,11,12,14,16,19,21,33,25,28
2	2,4,6,9,11,13,15,20,22,24,26,31
3	1,3,5,7,9,10,12,14,21,23,27,30
4	2,4,6,8,9,11,13,17,20,22,26,29,31
5	1,4,5,7,8,10,12,16,19,23,28
6	2,4,6,9,15,18,20,22,24,29
7	1,3,5,7,8,9,10,14,16,19,23,24,29
8	3,5,7,8,12,13,16,17,21,23,25,30
9	1,2,3,4,6,7,9,11,13,15,19,20,21,28,29,30

Specific Instances

Indian astrology, on which the system of *rashis* (mentioned earlier) depends, believes that the first letter of a name has a particular sound. Any letter having a friendly tone would sound agreeable, very much like music, especially Indian ragas which are embellished with appropriate *alapas* when sung. On the other hand, a discordant note shall spoil the musical pattern.

Suppose there is a person named Mohan, or Mohammad or Monnior. He shall have very agreeable relations with the persons of Dhanu *rashi* i.e., with persons whose names begin with Ye, Yo, Bha, Fa, Fra and so on, Bhaskar, Yogesha, Fazalbhai, or Francis, and the persons under Mesha *rashi*, i.e., those persons, the first letter of whose names is 'chu', 'la', etc., e.g., Chunnilal, Lal Khan, or Abraham, etc., besides his own *rashi*.

If we want to calculate the numbers of the letters of the names, we shall resort to the numerological basis. Let us consider the name 'Rakesh', which has the following number value:

R A K E S H
2 1 2 5 3 5 =18   =9

Let us compare it with
S A T I S H
3 1 4 1 3 5 =17   =8.

As 8 is a friendly number with respect to 9, it can be concluded that, on the whole, Rakesh shall have good relations with Satish. *We should not try to mix up both the systems, because then we shall only get confused. Let us choose one method at a time.* If we are fortunate enough to find out that both the systems recommend something common, then we must thank chance or providence.

Chapter 11

SOCIAL LIFE AND THE ASTROLOGICAL IMPORTANCE OF NAMES

Man has rightly been described as a social animal. He cannot survive without society. In fact, to be kept away from society is virtually a serious and unbecoming punishment that can be imposed on any person. However, nature has given adequate freedom to a person to choose his friends and partners. It is in this context that man can use his discretion and wisdom. As the famous philosopher Ecclesiasticus stated: "There is a friend, who is only a friend in name." On the other hand: "A faithful friend is the medicine of life" because "there is a friend that sticketh closer than a brother. R.W. Emerson has stated: "A friend is a person with whom I may be sincere. Before him I may think aloud." Shakespeare gives a correct description of a friend when he writes: "A friend should bear his friend's infirmities." A person without a friend is, in fact, very pitiable. Nicholas Breton has rightly written in his work *A Farewell to Town:* "I wish my deadly foe no worse/ Than want of friends, and empty purse."

One needs a lot of wisdom in selecting the right type of friend. Let us not forget the adage "that wisdom is more precious than rubies".

The term *friendship* should be understood in a very wide sense. Our marriage partnerships, business partnerships, political or social associations all come within the framework of friendship. Hence, it is necessary for us to be very choosy about them.

A family comes into existence as the result of the offspring generated by the union of a husband and a wife. If the husband or wife happens to belong to the category of undesirable persons, not only shall the married life be unhappy, but also the whole lineage shall be adversely affected.

According to genetics, the hereditary factors are present in the form of a cell — a single cell (the fertilized ovum) is $1/200''$ in diameter born as a result of the union of an ovum from the mother's ovary with a spermatozoon from the father. This single cell, in course of time, multiplies by division into millions of cells, becoming organs, muscles, glands, nerves, etc. We should bear in mind that genes, i.e., small structures occurring with the nucleus of all living cells are the real factors of an organism's development. These genes are contained in chromosomes which are, at times, called 'coloured bodies', because they become perceptible when the cell is stained by certain dyes. Generally, the number of chromosomes is constant for each species, but differs from one species to another. Each human cell contains 48 chromosomes (or 24 pairs), one chromosome of each pair being from the sperm and the other from the ovum.

When a cell divides, the 48 chromosomes 'split

longitudinally'. However, daughter cells and granddaughter cells and great-granddaughter cells, all down the line, "have exactly the same constitution as to chromosomes and genes as the original parent cell which started the individual off in life". Every gene is the vehicle of a unit character, i.e., hereditary factor which is invariably transmitted as a unit. Individuals differ hereditarily because genes can combine in innumerable patterns. Thus combinations of genes shall differ in the case of siblings, fraternal twins and so on. It has been estimated that a person gets half of his genes from each parent, a quarter of them from his grandparents, and 1/1024 of them from each ancestor ten generations back!

Apart from this hereditary influence, the influence of the environment too plays a vital role in the development of the human personality. The most important part of this environment is the home environment. The environment starts influencing a child right from the day he has been conceived. As long as the child is in the mother's womb, it is influenced by the mother. After birth, not only the mother and the father but other factors also try to exert their influence.

The following table reveals the extent of influence that heredity exercises:

Type of relationship	Correlation coefficient
Identical twins	0.90
Fraternal twins (both sexes)	0.70
Fraternal twins of unlike sex	0.59
Siblings	0.50
Parent and child	0.31
Cousins	0.27
Grandparent and grandchild	0.16
Unrelated children	0.00

The foregoing data should convince every sensible reader that one's marriage partner should be chosen carefully.

There is yet another type of friendship with which we all are acquainted. It is the friendship of the spirit, of the real selves, or due to the affinity of temperaments. In life, we make many friends, and although we think that we should not expect anything from them, we do expect at least a sense of sincerity. A friend who deceives us inevitably gives us a rude shock.

Some people are obliged to enter into business partnerships too. We all need money to sustain ourselves. In fact, neither religious merit nor happiness can be obtained without money (*dhanat dharma tatah sukham*). Consequently such partnerships have to be entered into very carefully, because lust for money may blind a person to resort to unethical conduct and prompt that person to throw even his friend out of a partnership. There is a saying that avarice of man is like a snake trying to swallow an elephant! The most precious commodity of the present age is sincerity.

The following observations throw light on the human nature:

The fishes, though deep in the water, may be hooked; the birds, though high in the air, may be shot; but man's secret thoughts are out of our reach.

The heavens may be measured; the earth may be surveyed; however the heart of man only is not to be known.

A man who has a beautiful soul always has some beautiful things to say, but a man who says beautiful things does not necessarily have a beautiful soul.

The virtuous will be sure to speak correctly, but those whose speech is good may not always be virtuous.

Men of principle are sure to be bold, but those who are bold may not always be men of principle.

In painting the tiger, you may delineate its skin but not its bones; in your acquaintance with a man, you may know his face but not his heart.

Thus, we find that great care has to be exercised in selecting every type of friend or partner, if a person wants to avoid the bitter experiences that may await him because of his want of proper discrimination.

Here, the help of astrology may be sought for determining the proper type of partner or friend. Astrology does not expect us to be idle or inactive. On the other hand, it is based on the principle that the effect of one's acts does not die but after one's life-time but extends even to future births. The Mimamsa school of Indian philosophy has propounded the theory that the effect generated from an act is, really speaking, indestructible. The horoscope is, therefore, the record of an individual's past (good or bad) deeds in a symbolic or code language, (*purva punayam likhyate janmapatrikā*). The Narada Purana states that nobody can evade the effect of one's good or bad acts (*avashyameva bhokktayyam kritam karma shubhāshubham*).

Indian philosophies such as the Sāmkhya and the Advaita believe in the theory of Satkrāyavada. This theory states that the cause itself is present in the form of the effect. We need not go into the details of this theory, but it is sufficient to note that many Indians do believe in the principle of action. They never advocate any theory of non-action or inaction or idleness.

The famous scientist Albert Einstein states the same fact in his own manner. "Events do not happen, they already exist, but can be seen on the time machine only." It is clear that our present life, our personality, character and temperament and related factors are caused by our past actions, rooted in past life. That is why we find differences and distinctions between the natures and temperaments of children belonging to the same family. Even an individual does not understand his own nature fully. The horoscope can indicate only the *fundamental nature* of that person. However, it is not possible to develop the correct or precise horoscope of every person. In the modern world of scientific developments, many persons do not believe in the efficacy of astrology. Hence, we have to rely on some other device through which we can understand something of the inherent nature of an individual. In this context the name of a person alone can provide some guidance.

Every word has its unique vibrations. It is worth noting that even in the ancient religions, word veneration was prevalent. The English poet Blake has expressed the 'word concept' in the verse (in *Songs of Experience*):

Hear the voice of the Bard
Who present, past, and future sees;
Whose ears have heard
The Holy Word
That walked among the ancient trees.
Tulasidasa, the noted Hindi poet and thinker, has

stated that the name of the lord is greater than the Lord Himself: (*Rāma te adhika Rama kara nama*).

The Psalms from the Bible declare: "Some trust in chariots, and some in horses: but we will remember the name of the Lord our God." Further, we have: "Where two or three are gathered together in my name, there am I in the midst of them" (Matthew 18:20).

The Eskimos also believe each person consists of three elements — body, soul and name.

The Taittiriya Brāhmana declares: "On the Spoken Word all the Gods depend, all beasts and men; in the Word live all creatures...the Word is the Imperishable, the firstborn of the eternal law, the mother of the Vedas, the navel of the divine world."

The power of the word or name was accepted by the ancient Egyptians too. An old Egyptian legend recounts how Isis, the great sorceress, craftily persuaded the Sun-God Ra to disclose his name to her, and how through possession of his name she gained power over him and over all other Gods.

There is a very close and essential identity between the word and what is denoted by it. This becomes clear not only from the objective standpoint, but also from the subjective one. We know from common experience that a person's ego, his very self and personality are indissolubly interlinked with that person's name. The name is not only a mere symbol, but is also a part of the personal possessions of its bearer. It is a property which one protects at any cost. In the ancient Roman law we find the concept of 'legal person'. Under that law no slave had any legal name, because he could not function as a legal person.

If we take away the name of a person, his entire

79

personality would suffer; his personal traits would be scattered because there shall be no uniting factor. The name functions as a proxy for its bearer and to utter the name may be considered equal to calling a person into being. The name is the real power. It is possible that the name is mystically connected with the personality of a person. Hence to understand a name may imply understanding the person to a certain extent. The name certainly has some suggestive power. A person becomes aggressive, when his name is interlinked with some undesirable thing, without any fault of his. According to G.K. Chesterton (in his *Song of Defeat*):

And we were angry and poor and happy,
And proud of seeing our names in print.

Even Lord Byron gives expression to a common universal human feeling: "'Tis pleasant, sure, to see one's name in print/A book's a book, although there's nothing in't."

Hence, for astrological purposes, we can rely to some extent on the name of a person to get an insight into his inner nature. Astrological devices, in a very mysterious, but yet scientific, way reveal the hidden traits of one's personality.

Although a person can always change himself to a certain extent, an ordinary person rarely tries to do so. He prefers his actions to be determined by his past. It takes time to change one's being completely. Moreover, it is impossible to change one's destiny, determined by the past, completely.

Hence, we should try to use astrological methodology to find out the possibilities of soundness of partnerships and friendships on the basis of names. It is just possible that we may not be able to know future events in totality with the help of astrology, yet we can get a glimpse of the future in more detail with the help of the astrological method than through ordinary common sense. Writing about astrology Yogi Aurobindo had stated in *Arya* (vol. 4, 1917-18, pp. 251-56):

Astrology is in the general mind associated with the class of subjects which goes under the name of the occult, and along with others of its class it has long been discredited by modern "enlightenment"; one does not quite know on what grounds or with what rational justification. It has its psychic and mystical side, but that is not its ordinary presentation; there it claims to be a science like any other with fixed processes and an exact and definite system of rules which ought to be perfectly capable of verification or of disproof by experiment and induction like any other science.

He has proceeded further to add very rightly:

It is not indeed the habit of educated Indians to profess explicitly their belief in it (i.e., astrology), they fight shy of that as a rule, but it is largely consulted by numbers of them, as also by many Europeans. This is an anomalous position which ought to be corrected. Either astrology is a true science and should be investigated, proved, improved where defective and generally rehabilitated in opinion, or else it is a pseudo-

science and should be investigated and disproved
so as to cut the ground away finally from all
secret belief or open credulity.

This is a very logical statement of truth about
astrology. In this context, this writer would like to
state that so far astrology has not been scientifically
disproved. On the other hand, it has been proved to
be true on the basis of empirical and logical truth. It
has to be admitted that there are charlatans too in the
domain of astrology; but such persons flourish
practically in every field. Can we say that there are no
charlatans in the domain of medicine? At one time,
quacks pervaded the medical field that the French
playwright Moliere was prompted to declare that
medicine is a 'gross pseudo-science'.

According to astrology planetary rays are unseen
vibrations that affect the physical, biological, and
psychological processes of a human being. These
vibrations emanate from solar energy. The ancient
seers could ascertain the importance of the Sun and
the energy emanating from it and its effect on the
earth, society and the individual. Indian astrology
gives the utmost importance to the Sun, the Moon and
other planets that exercise their influence in a silent
manner. Canl Jung has accepted the importance of
time, from the astrological standpoint when he stated:
"Whatever is born or done at this moment of time has
the qualities of this moment of time." That is why
astrology has been called the 'hora-shastra', i.e., the
science of time. It is also called *jyotisha*, i.e., the
science that discovers the influence of light. Astrology
is, in fact, a synthesis of physical, mental and natural
sciences, which makes it unique.

Attempts which have been honestly made to find out the veracity of astrology have revealed that astrology is a kind of science. For example, Kraft had published a work named '*Astro-physiologie*' in 1928. He presented a list of 72 persons who were born at around the same time. All these persons died at the same age and in a similar manner.

Symours studied the horoscopic charts of more than 100 centenarians and came to the conclusion that many of them had the zodiac signs Aries or Leo in ascendancy; that the 8th house was not generally tenanted; and the Sun and the Moon possessed only the beneficial aspects of Jupiter and Venus.

Several years ago Donald A. Bradley had published his work entitled *Profession and Birthdate*. This work contained a statistical analysis of the planetary positions found in the charts of 2492 eminent clergymen. Bradley has established that the positions of the Sun, the Moon, and the planets at the moment of birth have an important bearing on the personality of the individual and on his future.

Rufert Gleadow had published a systematic study of the horoscopes of 6960 eminent personalities. He established that planetary positions determined the profession of a person. For example, the position of the Sun in Aries or Libra makes a person successful in the political field. The Sun's position in Aquarias is good for a novelist while the position of the Sun in the Pisces makes a person proficient in mathematics.

As stated earlier in this chapter, we can easily get to know the name of a person. Hence, we have to find out the astrological implications of that name. In the ancient period, a *nama-karana sanskara* was performed, that is, a ceremony connected with giving a name to a child. That ceremony was important as the names were given on the basis of the birth charts. Now, of course, names are usually given at random. There is hardly any scientific attempt in giving names to children. Even then the names have some impact on the nature of the persons and they reveal the personalities of the individuals. For the benefit of those readers who intend to give names to their children on a scientific basis, we provide a chart based on *nakshatras* (stars).

Sl. No.	Nakshatras	Yoni	Gana	Nadi	Corresponding letters
1.	Ashvini	Ashva	Deva	Adya	chu-che-cho-la
2.	Bharani	Gaja	Manushya	Madhya	li-lu-le-lo
3.	Krittika	Mesha	Rakshasa	Antya	a-i-u-e
4	Rohini	Sarpa	Manushya	-do-	u-va-vi-vu
5.	Mrigashira	-do-	Deva	Aadya	ve-vo-ka-ki
6.	Aridra	Svana	Manushya	-do-	Ku-gha-da-ch-cha
7.	Poonarvasu	Marjara	Deva	-do-	ke-ko-ha-hi
8.	Pushya	Mesha	-do-	Madhya	hu-he-ho-da
9.	Ashlesha	Marjara	Rakshasa	Antya	di-du-de-do
10.	Makha	Mushak	-do-	-do-	ma-mi-mu-me
11.	PurvaPhalguni	-do-	Manushya	Madhya	mo-ta-ti-tu
12.	Uttara Phalgun	Gau	-do-	Adya	te-to-pa-pi
13.	Hasta	Mahishi	Deva	-do-	pu-sa-na-tha
14.	Chitta	Vyaghra	Rakshasa	Madhya	pa-po-ro-ri
15.	Swati	Mahishi	Deva	Antya	ru-re-ro-ta
16.	Visakha	Vyaghra	Rakshasa	-do-	ti-tu-te-to
17.	Anuradha	Mriga	Deva	Madhya	na-ni-nu-ne
18.	Jyashta	-do-	Rakshasa	Adya	no-ya-yi-yu
19.	Moola	Svana	-do-	-do-	ye-yo-bha-bhi
20.	Purva Ashadha	Kapi	Manushya	Madhya	bhu-dha-fa-dha
21.	UttaraAshadha	Babhru	-do-	Antya	bhe-bho-ja-ji
22.	Abhijit	-do-	-do-	-do-	ju-je-jo-kha
23.	Sharvana	Kapi	Deva	-do-	khi-khu-khe-kho
24.	Dhanishta	Simha	Rakshasa	Madhya	ga-gi-gu-ge
25.	Satabhisha	Ashva	-do-	Adya	go-sa-si-su
26.	Purva Bhadrapada	Simha	Manushya	-do-	se-so-da-di
27.	Uttara Bhadrapada	Gao	-do-	Madhya	du-jha-jaa-tha
28.	Revati	Hasti	Deva	Antya	cha-chi

On an astrological basis, the naming of a person was done by a fourfold method, viz. according to (1) the asterism under which a child was born, (2) the deity of the month, (3) the family deity, and (4) the popular name.

In the modern period, the aforementioned astrological basis is rarely followed. Hence, this basis has only a historical significance, although its importance cannot be underestimated.

Whatever the case, there is enough significance in the following statement of Brihaspati:

Name is the primary means of social intercourse; it brings about merit and is the root of fortune. Men attain fame from name. Therefore, naming ceremony is very praiseworthy.

(*Namakhila asya vyavaharahetuh subhavaham karmasu bhagyahetuh;*
namnaiva kirtim labhate manushyastataha
orasastam khalu namakarma.)

Chapter 12

INDICATION OF FUTURE POSSIBILITY
THROUGH PLAYING CARDS

By nature, human beings are inquisitive. They want to have a vision of the possible future events by any means. The growth of the popularity of astrology is a perfect example of this fact. While astrology seems to be based on some scientific data indicating the influences of visible stars or planets, other devices too have been exploited for astrological purposes.

We mention here the device of playing cards which have been used to determine the publicity of a future event occurring. How the cards are able to point to the future remains a mystery. But it is a fact that this writer's experience has shown that this device has sometimes given a correct indication of the future. This writer is reminded of the case of a person who approached an astrologer and asked him; "Shall I ever be able to have any issue?" The astrologer resorted to the playing cards device and predicted: "Yes, you shall definitely have more than one issue." This prediction proved to be correct.

The purpose of mentioning the playing cards' device is to give an opportunity to those readers who may be interested in using it to determine its credibility from their own experiences rather than depending on the views of others.

The following steps should now be followed:
1. Take a pack of playing cards.
2. Remove all twos, threes, fives and sixes and jokers.
3. Then we shall have the following cards in the pack:

(i)	sevens	4
(ii)	eights	4
(iii)	nines	4
(iv)	tens	4
(v)	jacks	4
(vi)	queens	4
(vii)	kings	4
(viii)	aces	4
	Total	32

4. Shuffle the cards and put them on the ground (face down).
5. Ask the questioner to state his question explicitly.
6. The question should be such as would yield a reply either in negative or positive terms. For example, one should not ask: 'When shall I get employment?' or 'When shall my brother return?'. Such questions cannot yield any answer through this device. But questions such as the following may be asked: 'Shall I be successful in this examination?' 'Shall I marry the girl I love?' 'Shall I get this employment?' 'Will my marriage take place within a year?' Thus any question which can

be answered either by a 'NO' or a 'YES' may be asked.

7. The questioner should then be asked to pick up one card from the pack.

   The nature of the card picked up shall reveal the answer. Also much will depend on whether the card picked up is 'heart', 'diamond', 'club' or 'spade'.

8. Now let us go into the details.

9. Suppose the card picked up is a heart. The following predictions may be made on the basis of the card:

Card	Indication (by way of prediction)
Ace	Complete success in love. Marriage in near future. Progress in business. Rise in fortune. Financial gain. Freedom from illness.
King	Love may increase still further. Possibility of marriage. Good opportunities in business. Gain of good fortune through efforts. Journey to other nations. Attainment of good health.
Queen	Pleasant turn in domestic life. Possibility of an early marriage. Favourable environment in business. Unexpected gain of money. Financial advancement. Betterment in health.
Jack	Obstacles in love. Delay in marriage. Government related problems in business. Harassing situation.
Ten	Good luck. Favourable period in love. It is not desirable to be very active in business; but possibility of amazing success.

Nine	Whatever desire you have in mind shall be fulfilled.Whatever question you have in mind shall be resolved satisfactorily.
Eight	Success in any undertaking. Possibility of an early journey. Some obstacles in love which, however, shall be removed in course of time. Beginning of a favourable period in financial matters.
Seven	Be careful in love matters. Possibility of acquiring a bad name. Financial problems. Difficulties in business.

If the card is a *spade* the following inferences are indicated:

Ace	Possibility of betrayal in love. Possibility of obstacles in marriage in near future. Loss in business. Problems in government-related matters.
King	The person whom you have trusted so far shall betray you. Marriage shall not take place soon; there shall be a long delay. Problems in business. Financial loss. Increased chances of illness.
Queen	Separation of the lover and the beloved in near future. Possibility of facing baseless allegations. Possibility of additional delay in marriage. The coming period not favourable for financial matters. Problems in business. Poor health indicated.
Jack	It would be better to forget about love affairs for some time. Moderate business period. Unexpected financial loss.

Ten	Coming period not favourable. Hence, all activities to be undertaken after much consideration and cool thinking. Continuous obstacles in business. Possibility of financial loss. Period unfavourable for physical health.
Nine	It would be better to forget the golden period that you have enjoyed. Forget that you had once witnessed a very lovable period. The coming period may bring loss, insinuation, neglect and harassment.
Eight	Implement your plans very carefully, the time is not favourable. The coming period shall remain unfavourable for a pretty long time.
Seven	Time is unfavourable from every point of view. Bad period for love-making; it may bring you disgrace. Married life being full of agony is a possibility.

If the card is a *diamond*, the following indications should be noted:

Ace	The desire you entertain at present shall be fulfilled in the near future. You shall shortly receive an important letter.
King	Within some days, you shall meet a person who can be said to be competent and who is important to you. He shall prove helpful to you.
Queen	Be watchful and do not allow rumours concerning yourself to spread. These rumours may cause unnecessary trouble.

Jack	Possibility of a journey in the near future. The journey shall be helpful in fulfilling your cherished objective.
Ten	Possibility of a change in your present life pattern. This change is likely to prove favourable. Unexpected financial gain is indicated.
Nine	Pleasant news about a person very close to you. Unexpected and sudden chance in business.
Eight	You shall undertake a cherished journey in the near future. Also, remarkable gain in the near future.
Seven	Possibility of a sudden gain through lottery, meeting or reward. The various problems shall be solved within a couple of days.

If the card is a *club*, then the following indications deserve notice:

Ace	Remarkable success in financial matters possible. Likely to get pleasant news from your life-partner.
King	Cast off fear and suspicion from your heart. Whatever plan you have prepared becomes quite workable; you shall shortly get good results.
Queen	You may establish a relation with a wealthy widow or widower. You may be a gainer in business; exploit the opportunity.

Jack	You may come in contact with a new girl or youth. The relation may become stronger in course of time.
Ten	Unexpected gain of money. Unexpected journey. Unexpected success at work.
Nine	You are likely to be married to a beautiful handsome and lovely person. You may obtain ample financial gain from this union. The desire of your heart too shall be fulfilled.
Eight	Possibility of rise in fortunes. Golden future indicated. Strive to move forward; you shall positively gain success.
Seven	The coming period is favourable from all angles. Remarkable financial gain possible. Increase in business. Freedom from disease. Victory in a court case. Time to fulfil heart's desires.

Chapter 13

SIGNIFICANT INDICATIONS OF THE HAND AND THE PALM

The lines found in an individual's palm give a clue to his nature and also provide a broad outline of his future. Sometimes, a horoscope may be incorrect due to the wrong time of birth being taken into account or due to defects in the watch. The result is that because of such wrong factors the entire horoscope may be incorrect and the prediction based on this wrong horoscope may be incorrect and the prediction based on this wrong horoscope could also be wrong. Many times, therefore, the predictions made about a person's future prove to be wrong, which is a matter of common experience. But the fault lies in the horoscope cast and not in the science of astrology. Wrong data can yield only a wrong result just as, in logic, one cannot reach a true conclusion on the basis of wrong premises.

In one case, which came to this writer's notice, the horoscopes of the boy and the girl were duly matched before their marriage; but the girl became

95

a widow within a short period.

The untimely demise of Rajiv Gandhi is a case in point. Many astrologers predicted that he would become the Prime Minister of India once again after the May 1991 elections. But in reality he lost his life in a bomb blast in May 1991.

Both these cases reveal that the fault lies in the horoscope and not in its astrological interpretation.

For leading a successful married life as well as for achieving a successful business partnership or friendship, one needs an adjusting nature and an ideal and happy combination of the qualities of the head as well as of the heart. A reading of hands can be very helpful in cases where the correctness of a horoscope is doubtful.

In this context, let us acquaint ourselves with the most significant aspects of the palm. Besides the lines, other factors such as the shape of the hand, the colour of the hand, the shape of the fingers and the thumb, and related signs, too, have their own importance. And all these indications have to be analysed and synthesized before proper prediction can be made. Since it is very easy to see the lines on palm, these lines alone may signify the basic trait of an individual.

Before we take up a discussion of the lines on the hands, let us acquaint ourselves with the positions of mounts on the palm. A mount is present inside a hand, a little below the place where the fingers are connected with the palm, in the shape of slight swellings.

Key Diagram: Points on the Hands

1   Fingertips
2   Fingers
3   Phalanges
4   Thumb
5   Life line
6   Head line
7   Heart line
8   Fate line
9   Sun line
10 Mercury line
11 Line of love and affection
12 Mount of Venus
13 Mount of the Moon
14 Mount of Mars
15 Mount of Jupiter
16 Mount of Saturn
17 Mount of Apollo
18 Mount of Mercury

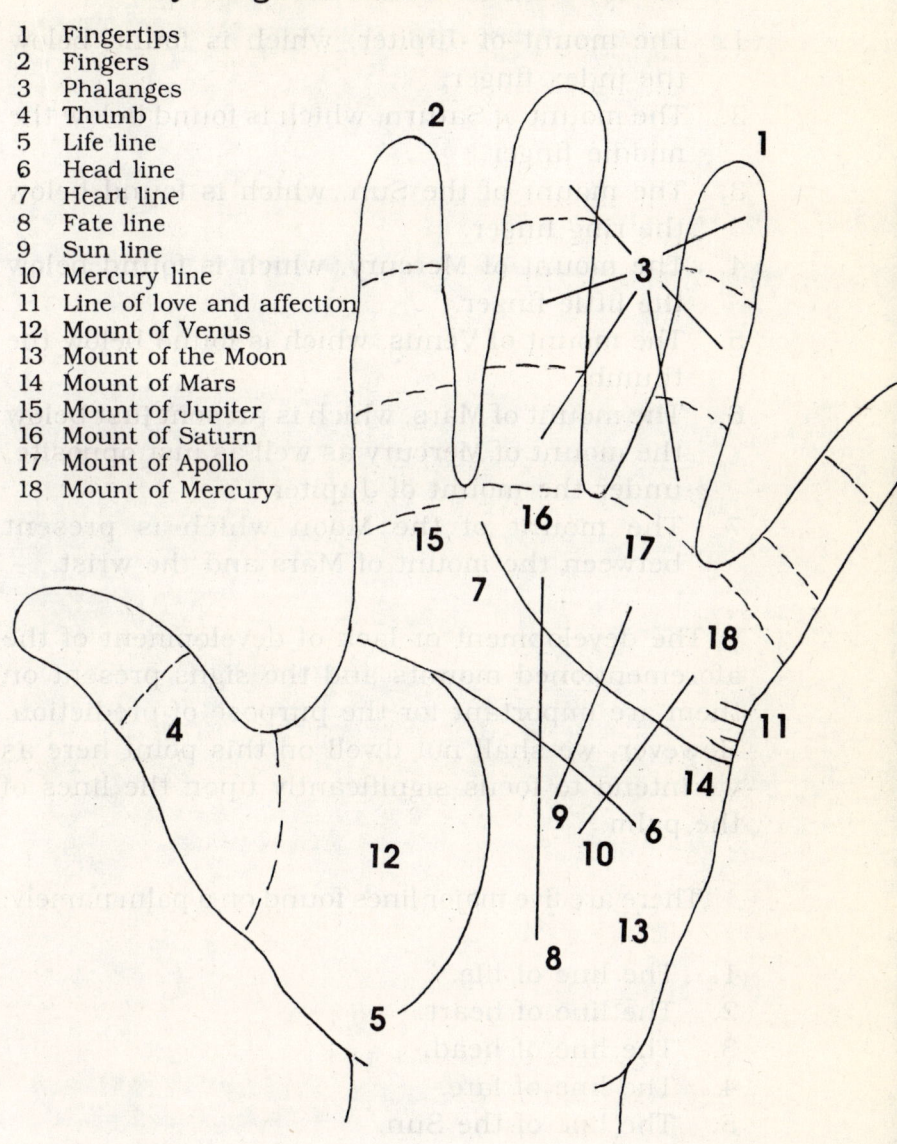

The names of these mounts are stated as follows:

1. The mount of Jupiter, which is found below the index finger.
2. The mount of Saturn, which is found below the middle finger.
3. The mount of the Sun, which is found below the ring finger.
4. The mount of Mercury, which is found below the little finger.
5. The mount of Venus, which is found below the thumb.
6. The mount of Mars, which is present just below the mount of Mercury as well as just opposite, under the mount of Jupiter.
7. The mount of the Moon which is present between the mount of Mars and the wrist.

The development or lack of development of the aforementioned mounts and the signs present on them are important for the purpose of prediction. However, we shall not dwell on this point here as we intend to focus significantly upon the lines of the palm.

There are five major lines found on a palm namely:

1. The line of life.
2. The line of heart.
3. The line of head.
4. The line of fate.
5. The line of the Sun.

There are, undoubtedly, other important lines too. But we shall not discuss them here as our objective is limited to determining whether a person can prove to be a faithful and a fortunate partner.

The Line of Life

The line of life is the most important line as life is the most important entity for everybody. This line is found at the base of the mount of Venus. This line should be clear, distinct, long and free from any cross or break.

If the life line is pale and flat (broad), ill health, bad habits and a weak and envious character are indicated.

If the life line is thick and red, a violent and brutal mentality is indicated. A chained and linked life line indicates delicacy of health.

If this line appears as a big circle in the palm of the hand and reaches or ends close to the Mount of the Moon, a long life is indicated.

If this line commences under the Mount of Jupiter, this is a sign of great ambition and achievement of and success in life.

If this line stops abruptly, this is a sign of a sudden death, and any break in this line is an indication of possible illness.

If this line is very close to the line of the head, this is an indication of a life guided by reason and prudence.

If there is a medium space between the life line and the line of the head, this is an indication of a pushing nature, but shows a lack of prudence.

If a fork of the life line goes into the line of the head, faithfulness is indicated.

In short, the life line should be free from any defect. A strong life line is the biggest asset of any human being. If the life line is accompanied by a strong sister line, very good health is certain.

Line of the Head

The importance of the line of the head is clear from its name itself. This line is found under the line of the heart, running almost parallel to it. A long, straight and clear head line is an indication of robust common sense.

Well-developed head line, with good mounts of Jupiter and Mercury, is an indication of the presence of concentration power.

A long and straight head line, with a good line of heart, is an indication of the presence of the quality of tactfulness.

A narrow and weak head line is an indication of frivolity, and a chained head line indicates the occurrence of headaches.

A short head line with a depressed mount of Jupiter indicates laziness.

A head line running only half way across the palm is a sign of lack of intelligence.

If the head line is not joined with the life line at the start, this is a sign of self-reliance.

If the head line is far apart from the line of life at the start and the mount of Mercury is very flat, these factors show a streak of recklessness.

If the head line is long and slopes towards the mount of the Moon and the mount of Jupiter is high, the quality of eloquence is indicated.

If the head line ends just before it crosses the line of fate, this is an indication of short life.

If the head line is long and clear and terminates on the lower mount of Mars, presence of mind is indicated.

If the head line is closely connected for some distance with the line of life, diffidence is indicated.

If the head line has a sister head line, this is a sign of good thinking power.

The Line of the Heart

The line of the heart is a horizontal line that runs across the palm at the base of the mounts.

A long, clear and well-formed heart line indicates lasting affection. If this line streches clear across the hand, it denotes blind affection.

A double line of heart shows a capacity for deep affection, which could result in sorrow for the possesor.

If the heart line starts from the third phalanx of the first finger, this is an indication of lack of success.

If the heart line starts from under the mount of Saturn, this indicates sensuality and affection.

A weak and poorly formed heart line indicates faithlessness.

A chained heart line is an indication of flirtatious disposition.

A much broken heart line indicates inconsistency in love.

The absence of a heart line is a sign of physical coldness, selfishness and avarice.

If the heart line is well developed and the mounts of Venus and the Moon are unduly developed, these features indicate romantic nature.

If the heart line is cut under the mount of Mercury by another line, this is an indication of business failure.

Lines running from the line of the heart to the

line of the head, without touching the latter, indicate a life greatly influenced by the opposite sex.

If the heart line starts from the mount of Jupiter and is connected with a straight, clear line of fate coming from the mount of the Moon, this is an indication of unexpected happiness.

We may summarize the main features of the heart line by stating that a long, clear and distinct heart line is a great asset for any individual.

The Line of Fate

The line of fate starts in the lower part of palm and usually terminates at the roots of the fingers.

If this line runs directly to the mount of the Sun, fame is indicated.

The absence of a fate line is a sign of an insignificant life.

If the fate line rises from the *Rascette* (wrist) and runs to the third phalanx of the second finger, it is a sign of outstanding destiny.

If this line starts from the mount of Moon and runs to the second finger, a rise through self-effort is indicated.

If the fate line is poorly formed and terminates abruptly at the line of the head in both hands, misfortune is indicated.

If the fate line is broken, each break indicates some change in one's life pattern.

If the fate line as well as life line are intersected by many lines, cutting them horizontally, this is an indication of grief.

If the fate line rises from the line of life and the mounts of Jupiter and Venus are well developed, a spirit of benevolence is indicated.

102

If the fate line is chained when it crosses the line of the heart, this is an indication of trouble in love.

If the line of fate is broken and cut by many small lines, this is an indication of continued misfortune.

If any branch of the fate line moves to the mount of the Sun, a gain of wealth is indicated.

Crosses on the fate line indicate pecuniary difficulties.

If the line of fate starts in a zigzag manner or with a series of crosses, this is an indication of a trouble-some childhood.

If there is a cross on the fate line, this is an indication of a change in the life pattern.

A clean, long and distinct fate line is an indication of good fortune.

The Sun Line

Generally, the Sun line starts low down in the palm and it terminates on the mount of the Sun; hence its name.

A well-formed Sun line in both the hands indicates success in every endeavour.

If the Sun line is long and is not intersected by any other line, this indicates inflow of money.

If the sun line is deep and the mount of Jupiter is well developed in both hands, this indicates good relations with highly placed persons.

If this line is found to be broken repeatedly, the indication is that the subject may be versatile, but shall not be able to achieve success or a good reputation in the financial field.

If the Sun line rises from the line of life, this denotes success in art. If the Sun line is cut by the marriage line, loss of social status due to an unsuitable marriage is indicated.

If there are two deep sun lines, this is an indication of glory and unexpected success.

We can conclude this discussion by stating that a study of palm lines may reveal the basic personality of a person. As nobody can hide his or her hand for long, it is possible to judge a person's personality easily.

It should be remembered that the aforementioned study can yield only a probable estimate or outline of a personality. A probable outline of personality is better than no outline at all. Hence, such a study has its own utility and significance.

The Thumb

The thumb has its own importance. In fact, one author has even declared that: "The higher animal is revealed in the hand, but the man is in the thumb."

According to law, if a person is not literate, his or her thumb impression is accepted as a substitute for a signature.

A large thumb indicates that the person cannot be influenced easily. Such a person is thoughtful and relies on his own thinking rather than on anybody else's suggestions or opinions.

On the other hand, a small thumb indicates that the subject can be easily influenced. Such a person is ruled by the heart and not by the head. However, what is more important to be noted is whether a thumb is flexible or not. A stiff thumb, which can be bent only very little, indicates stubbornness. Such a person cares a fig for the emotions of others and has a tendency to limit himself to his family.

On the contrary, if the thumb is flexible, i.e., if it bends back easily, this indicates that a person is adaptable by nature and cares for the feelings of others.

Too much flexibility of the thumb, however, is not a good sign. A person with such a thumb would have no principles in life.

While developing friendship, it is desirable to establish relations with a person who has flexible attitude. In the absence of such an adjusting capacity, it is difficult to maintain relations for long.

All the indications or features mentioned earlier are broad ones. One must be intelligent enough to understand their significance and implication, in specific instances, while dealing with others.

Chapter 14

SOME INDICATIONS FROM THE FACE

An individual's personality reveals itself to some extent through the face too. This is obvious from our individual experiences. For instance when we meet a particular person, we feel that 'he appears to be a nice man'. However, when we meet another person, we feel that he does not appear to be 'good.'

In this context, we would like to emphasize the point that face reading is not science; it is a matter of intuitive experience. However, sometimes certain facial characteristics and physical features help us in understanding a stranger to some extent.

Body Build

A slender person is likely to be sensitive, intellectually sharp, emotional, imaginative and creative in outlook. Such persons are generally not fit for business or political activity which requires a great deal of manipulating skill.

On the other hand, fat persons are generally

jovial and friendly. They are kind-hearted and fond of earthly pleasures.

Square and Triangular Faces

A person with square face is normally full of self-confidence. He is by nature very practical and can do well in any profession concerned or dealing with a large public.

A triangular face, on the other hand, indicates an intellectual or a dreamer. Such a person is shy by nature. A person with such a face can be successful in the domains of philosophy, art, music and so on.

Forehead

A high and wide forehead is an indication of intelligence and vitality. Such a forehead elicits positive responses from people and, therefore, can be taken to be a sign of success in life.

One wrinkle on the forehead indicates a greedy nature. But it also indicates that the person shall shine as a result of sheer hard work.

Two wrinkles on the forehead indicate two important areas of life viz. the area of personal relations with others and the area of health and popularity.

If the upper line (wrinkle) is shorter and thinner than the lower one, this indicates that such a person cannot depend on his associates. If the lower line is long and deep, this is an indication of popularity and success.

If there are three wrinkles on the forehead, they indicate perception and good memory. The deep lines indicate the extent of worry that the person has endured. However, three lines generally indicate a successful person.

Total absence of wrinkles is an indication that a person would achieve success during middle age, i.e., after thirty-five or so.

Eyes

Eyes that possess sparkle and brilliance indicate that the person is kind-hearted.

Large eyes are signs of an artistic and sentimental nature. They also indicate a moody nature.

Persons with small eyes are practical and strong-willed. They do not follow anybody blindly.

Nose

The size and shape of one's nose show one's ability to prosper and also one's sense of culture and sentiment.

The length of one's nose should ideally be one-third the length of one's face. If a nose falls short of this length, it is considered short, and if a nose exceeds this length, it is considered long.

A short nose is an indication of an adaptable and open-hearted temperament. Such a nose indicates that its possessor is usually not interested in deeper aspects of life.

A long nose indicates refined taste and a sense of responsibility.

Persons with long noses are sincere workers. However, an excessively long nose is an indication of unpractical nature. Small nose with nostril wings is considered good for success in business. Persons with such noses rise from humble positions to high ones by sheer dint of their labour and business acumen.

Mouth

The mouth can reveal a person's attitude towards various facets of life including food. A large mouth indicates that the person likes to lead a comfortable life, that is, he is fond of luxuries.

A small mouth is an indication of a timid and sentimental nature.

Further, a person with a small mouth is likely to be highly self-centred.

A smiling mouth indicates a gentle and friendly nature.

Ears

Large ears indicate a spirit of courage and dashingness. They also indicate a long life.

Small ears indicate an artistic tendency. The talent possessed by persons with small ears attain development rather late in life.

Ears which are large in the upper part indicate intelligence and good memory.

Ears whose lower portions are large indicate a personality that is jovial and gay.

Wrinkles on the cheeks

Two wrinkles, radiating from the nose and going downwards indicate a sense of responsibility and hard work.

Absence of wrinkles on the cheeks in the case of adults indicates instability in work. Such a person is likely to make frequent changes in his job.

The reader is warned that the indications mentioned here should not be accepted as sure or accurate guides in an assessment of an individual's personality.

Chapter 15

BIRTH DATE GUIDE

Sometimes, it may happen that one knows the birth date of a person with whom one wants to transact business or establish some other kind of relationship. Naturally, one would like the relationship to be cordial and long lasting.

According to the Gregorian calendar, the Sun remains in the following *rashis* of the zodiac during the period specified against each:

1	Aries	21 March to 20 April
2	Taurus	21 April to 20 May
3	Gemini	21 May to 20 June
4	Cancer	21 June to 20 July
5	Leo	21 July to 20 August
6	Virgo	21 August to 23 September
7	Libra	24 September to 23 October
8	Scorpio	24 October to 22 November
9	Sagittarius	23 November to 20 December
10	Capricorn	21 December to 19 January
11	Aquarius	20 January to 18 February
12	Pisces	19 February to March 20

But as far as the Indian calendar is concerned, the Sun stays in the following *rashis* during the period mentioned against each. As we are following Indian system here, it would be more appropriate to follow the Indian calendar:

1.	Mesh	15 April to 14 May
2.	Vrishabha	15 May to 14 June
3.	Mithuna	15 June to 14 July
4.	Karka	15 July to 14 August
5.	Simha	15 August to 14 September
6.	Kanya	15 September to 14 October
7.	Tula	15 October to 14 November
8.	Vrishchika	15 November to 14 December
9.	Dhanu	15 December to 14 January
10.	Makara	15 January to 14 February
11.	Kumbha	15 February to 14 March
12.	Meena	15 March to 14 April

According to Indian astrology, the Sun represents the soul of the Cosmic Being, while the Moon represents the mind of Cosmic Being. These factors indicate that one can infer about the spiritual tendency of a person from the position of the Sun in his ascendant (*lagna*). The mind is, of course, affected by the spiritual tendency. It may, therefore, be worthwhile to consider the position of the Sun, too, if possible. This implies that if one studies the Ravi (Sun) *rashi* as well as the Chandra (Moon) *rashi* of a person, a clearer picture of a person's personality can be obtained rather than by merely clinging to the Chandra *rashi* or the name alone. Of course it is not always necessary to go after a person's birth date, because this may not be possible at times. In such a situation, the name can be relied upon to a certain extent. Wherever it is possible to know both the name as well as the birth date, both Chandra *rashi* as well as the Ravi *rashi* can be consulted.

If the Sun is in Mesha, a person is likely to be a follower of certain principles rigidly. He is also likely to be assertive, susceptible to anger, outspoken, courageous, ambitious, liberal-minded, disciplined, dominating, critical and reliable.

If the Sun is in Vrishabha, a person is likely to be practical, consistent, and self-reliant. He is very industrious and persistent. He is consistent in his affection and is generally free from anger. But he flies into a rage due to certain reasons, it is difficult to calm down his anger, which has a tendency to linger.

If the Sun is in Mithuna, such a position makes a person persuasive, creative, sensitive, expressive and practical. Such a person's mind is full of ideas and is devoted to learning, and he is an expert in conversation and is quick-witted.

If the Sun is in Karka this makes a person social, affectionate, sensitive, cautious, fickle-minded, efficient, and helpful. Such a person tries to keep his word.

If the Sun is in Simha, this makes a person fearless, liberal, egoistic, honest, independent, and unselfish in conduct. Such a person is likely to become a good administrator and a leader in any walk of life.

If the Sun is in Kanya, this makes a person realistic, disciplined, receptive to ideas, analytical, methodical, argumentative, rational, practical, and modest. Such a person makes a good manager. This person cannot be deceived easily and has a natural business acumen.

If the Sun is in Tula, this makes a person friendly, humorous and sympathetic. Such a person can make adjustments in life. He is discriminating in nature, but his ideas are not stable.

If the Sun is in Vrishchika, this makes a person selective, strong-minded, practical and courageous. However, it also makes him greedy and shorttempered. He cannot easily forgive a person who offends him. He is likely to be a good speaker and organiser.

If the Sun is in Dhanu, it makes a person wise and discriminating. Such a person proves successful to a certain extent in his undertakings, because he is reliable and charismatic. He is always active and possesses a fertile mind. He loves justice and is frank. He constantly seeks fame and a good reputation. He is likely to be miserly and loves saving money to the extent possible.

If the Sun is in Makara, this makes a person calculating, quarrelsome and tedious. Such a person can take sensible decisions, but is impatient. He is extremely particular about time and work, but he is likely to be wilful to certain extent.

If the Sun is in Kumbha, this makes a person sensitive, individualistic, and rebellious. But such a person can make friends easily. He is lazy but truthful. He never divulges his secrets completely. He is efficient and faces the chances of being deceived by unexpected quarters.

If the Sun is in Meena, this makes a person optimistic, wise and discriminating. He gains popularity and fame without much effort. Such a person is pious in habits and attitudes.

Relationship with other *rashis*

If your Sun is in Mesha, you are likely to have fruitful relations with persons whose Sun is in Simha, Dhanu or Kumbha.

If your Sun is in Vrishabha, you are likely to have fruitful relations with persons whose Sun is in Kanya, Makara or Meena.

If your Sun is in Mithuna, you are likely to have fruitful relations with persons whose Sun is in Tula, Kumbha or Mesha.

If your Sun is in Karka, you are likely to have fruitful relations with persons whose Sun is in Vrishchika, Meena or Vrishabha.

If your Sun is in Simha, you are likely to have fruitful relations with persons whose Sun is in Dhanu, Mesha or Mithuna.

If your Sun is in Kanya, you are likely to have fruitful relations with persons whose Sun is in Makara, Vrishabha or Karka.

If your Sun is in Tula, you are likely to have fruitful relations with persons whose Sun is in Kumbha, Mithuna or Simha.

If your Sun is in Vrishchika, you are likely to have fruitful relations with persons whose Sun is in Meena, Karka or Kanya.

If your Sun is in Dhanu, you are likely to have fruitful relations with persons whose Sun is in Mesha, Simha or Tula.

If your Sun is in Makara, you are likely to have fruitful relations with persons whose Sun is in Vrishabha, Kanya or Vrishchika.

If your Sun is in Kumbha, you are likely to have fruitful relations with persons whose Sun is in Mithuna, Tula or Dhanu.

If your Sun is in Meena, you are likely to have fruitful relations with persons whose Sun is in Karka, Vrishchika or Makara.

The foregoing details can be illustrated through the following chart for obtaining guidance at a glance:

Your Ravi (Surya) *rashi*	The corresponding friendly Surya *rashis*
1. Mesha	Simha, Dhanu, Kumbha
2. Vrishabha	Kanya, Makara, Meena
3. Mithuna	Tula, Kumbha, Mesha
4. Karka	Vrishchika, Meena, Vrishabha
5. Simha	Dhanu, Mesha, Mithuna
6. Kanya	Makara, Vrishabha, Karka
7. Tula	Kumbha, Mithuna, Simha
8. Vrishchika	Meena, Karka, Kanya
9. Dhanu	Mesha, Simha, Tula
10. Makara	Vrishabha, Kanya, Vrishchika
11. Kumbha	Mithuna, Tula, Dhanu
12. Meena	Karka, Vrishchika, Makara.

Root Number and the Fortunate Dates

Usually persons are keen to know the dates on which they should begin any work or job they intend to undertake. An astrologer is generally consulted to find out the favourable dates. However, it is possible to determine the favourable dates with the help of root numbers too. Of course, it is a matter of faith to choose this alternative.

The root number is obtained by reducing the birth date to a single unit. For example, suppose the birth date of Mr. X is 26-12-1927.

This birth date can be reduced to one unit in the following manner:

116

Date: 26 (2+6) =8
Month: 12 (1+2) =3
Year 1927 (1+9+2+7) =(1+9) = (1+0) =1
Total = 12, i.e., (1+2) 3

Thus the root number obtained is 3. Everybody can calculate his or her root number in the manner just explained.

Now, we tabulate the lucky days for each root number, as follows:

Root number	Lucky days of every month
1	1, 5, 14 and 23
2	2, 6, 15 and 24
3	3, 7, 16 and 25
4	4, 8, 17 and 26
5	5, 9, 18 and 27
6	1, 5, 6, 10, 19 and 24
7	2, 7, 11, 20 and 29
8	3, 8, 12, 21 and 30
9	4, 9, 13, 22 and 31

Appendix 1

FAVOURABLE TIMES

The favourable time for beginning any activity can be determined with the help of the following chart to some extent:

Day Time (beginning from morning)

Sun	9-10.30	10.30-12	1.30-3	
Mon	6-7.30	9-10.30	3-4.30	4.30-6
Tue	10.30-12	12-1.30	3-4.30	
Wed	6-7.30	7.30-9	10.30-12	4.30-6
Thu	6-7.30	12-1.30	4.30-6	
Fri	7.30-10.30		12-1.30	
Sat	7.30-9	1.30-3	3-4.30	

Night Time (beginning from 6 p.m. (to dawn)

Sun	6-9	1.30.3	4.30-6	
Mon	10.30-12	1.30-3	3-4.30	
Tue	7.30-9	10.30-1.30		
Wed	7.30-9	9-10.30	3-4.30	
Thur	6-7.90	12-1.30	3-6	
Fri	9-10.30	12-3		
Sat	6-7.30	9-10.30	10.30-12	4.30-6

Appendix 2

SOME NUMEROLOGICAL METHODS

Though from an astrological viewpoint the following two methods for ascertaining whether or not one shall attain success in an endeavour may not be justified, they have been traditionally used by certain people rather satisfactorily and are described here. A person desirous of knowing the fate of his effort may try any one of the two methods.

Method I
The relevant number chart is depicted as follows:

5	4	3	2	1
6	7	8	9	10
15	14	13	12	11
16	17	18	19	20

A person desirous of knowing the answer to his question (in a serious manner) should place the index figure of his right hand (or any other pointed object) (with his eyes closed) after remembering his favourite deity, in one of the aforementioned houses. The result can be judged on the following basis:

1. Success in his effort.
2. Success and the end of sorrow.
3. Success and profit.
4. Failure.
5. Success of a moderate nature.
6. Good success.
7. Excellent success.
8. No hope of success.
9. Advantage and success.
10. Advantage and success.
11. Success.
12. Failure.
13. Failure.
14. Success.
15. Success.
16. Doubtful success.
17. Success and happiness.
18. Moderate success i.e., 50 per cent chance of success.
19. Success cannot be certain.
20. Success.

Method 2

Think of any number ranging from 1 to 108. Divide it by 12. The reminder figures indicate the following:

1,9,7	Success after some delay.
8,8,10,5	Failure.
11	Success.
2	Advancement.
3,6,12,0	Success is imminent.

The foregoing chart can help a person in understanding the effects of the transits of different planets through the *rashi* of a person. However, the results indicated should not be taken as certainties; only probability is indicated. A chart is not a simple item that can be completely grasped at a glance. It has to be interpreted in a synthetic and integrative manner. However, the effects indicated can be accepted as the eventualities that could happen and due precautions may be taken to avert the adverse effects of such eventualities and efforts may be made to achieve maximum advantage when the time is favourable.

Appendix 3

INFLUENCE OF TRANSITS OF PLANETS

There may be some readers who are interested in knowing the influence of the transit of the planets in the different houses of their *rashi chakra*, i.e., the horoscope based on *rashi*. For them the following details may be useful.

House	Surya	Chandra	Bhauma	Budha	Brihaspati	Shukra	Shani	Rahu	Ketu
	I	II	III	IV	V	VI	VII	VIII	IX
1.	Sthananasha (displacement)	Pushti and annalabha (nourishment and gain of food)	Bhayam and pida (fear and agony)	Bandhana + bhayam (fear of imprisonment)	Arishtadibhayam (fear of impediments)	Sukham and shatrunashah (happiness and elimination of enemies)	Sarvahanih and pidabhayam (loss and fear of agony)	Hanih and kashtam (loss and difficulty)	Hanih and rogabhayam (loss and fear of disease)
2.	Hanih and bhayam (loss and fear)	Dhanalabha and sukham (attainment of money and happiness)	Dhananashah and netrartih (loss of money and eye trouble)	Dhanalabhah (gain of money)	Dhanadilabhah (gain of money etc.)	Sukham and arthalabha (happiness and gain of money)	Shokah and dhanahanih (unhappiness and loss of money)	Naihsvam and vyayam (dejection and expenses)	Vairam and vittanasham (enmity and expenses)
3.	Sukham and shripraptih (happiness and attainment of money and fame)	Dravyaprapti and sukham (monetary gain and happiness)	Sukham and shripraptih (happiness and attainment of success)	Shatruto-bhayam (danger from the enemy)	Bhayam and rogapraptih (fear and danger of illness)	Sukham and arthapraptih (happiness and money gain)	Sukharthalabhah (attainment of money and happiness)	Nairujjam and dhanapraptih (freedom from disease and monetary gain)	Sukhalabha and vriddhih (attainment of happiness and progress)
4.	Rogabhayam and Mananashah (fear of disease and danger to prestige)	Rogabhayartha-siddhih (danger of illness, procurement of money)	Kashtam and shatgrubhitih (difficulties and fear of enemies)	Dhanasukha-praptih (attainment of money and happiness)	Dhanahanir vyayam (loss of money and expenses)	Dhanagamah (inflow of money)	Pidabhayam and shatruviriddhih (fear of suffering; increase of enemies)	Vairam and shokam (enmity and dejection)	Bhitih and pida (fear and suffering)
5.	Dainyam and hanih (humiliation and loss)	Sukham and karyanashah (happiness and negation of action)	Rogabhayam and dananashah (danger of illness and loss of money)	Rogah and shokah (illness and sorrow)	Labhah and sukhamcha (gain and happiness)	Labhah and putralabhah (monetary gain and gain of progeny)	Dhanaputrayoh and pida (suffering with respect to wealth and progeny)	Hanih and shokashcha (loss and sorrow)	Shokah and arthanashah (grief and loss of money)

House	Surya	Chandra	Bhauma	Budha	Brihaspati	Shudra	Shani	Rahu	Ketu
	I	II	III	IV	V	VI	VII	VIII	IX
6.	*Ripunashah* and *sukham* (destruction of enemies and happiness)	*Vittalabhah* (gain of money)	*Sukharthalabhah* (happiness and monetary gain)	*Albhasthitih* (state of no gain)	*Rogah* and *shokashcha* (illness and sorrow)	*Shatruvriddhih* and *pidacha* (increase of enemies and suffering)	*Sukham* and *vittalabhah* (happiness and monetary gain)	*Sukham* and *lakshamipraptih* (gain of happiness and prosperity)	*Sukhavittadan* (attainment of happiness and money)
7	*Gamanam* and *dhanahanih* (journey and loss of money)	*Dravyapraptih* and *sukham* (attainment of money and happiness)	*Karashyam* and *dhananashah* (feebleness or weakness and loss of money)	*Pidabhayam* and *vigrahah* (danger of suffering and conflict)	*Sammanam* and *sukhamcha* (prestige and happiness)	*Shokah* and *bhayam* (grief and fear)	*Doshah* and *pidabhayam* (allegations and danger of suffering)	*Hanih* and *kalahah* (loss and wrangling)	*Durgatih* and *pidacha* (bad conditions and suffering)
8.	*Rogaptih* and *bhayam* (illness and fear)	*Kleshbhayam* (danger of acute suffering)	*Bhayam* and *papavriddhih* (fear and increase in sin)	*Annadilabhah* (gain of food, etc.)	*Jivabhayam* and *shokam* (danger to life and suffering)	*Vippattih* and *dhanakshyayah* (adversity and loss of money)	*Pidabhayam* and *shatruvriddhihi* (fear of suffering and increase of enemies)	*Bhayam* and *sukhamcha* (fear and happiness)	*Pidabhayam* and *hanihshcha* (fear of suffering and loss)
9.	*Kantikshayah* and *papabuddhih* (increase in lustre and evil thoughts)	*Manam* and *nripabhayam* (renown and fear from government)	*Rogabhayam* (danger of illness)	*Rogabhayam* and *dhananashah* (danger of illness and loss of money)	*Sukham* and *Sammanam* (happiness and reputation)	*Sukham* and *labhah* (happiness and gain)	*Papam* and *dhananashah* (evil act and destruction of wealth)	*Papakarmaratih* (involvement in an evil act)	*Papam dainyashcha* (evil acts and humiliation)
10.	*Saukhyam* and *karmasiddhih* (happiness and success in endeavour)	*Shubham, sukham* (auspicious act and happiness)	*Sukham* and *shokashcha* (happiness and sorrow)	*Sukham* and *sukhabhogah* (happiness and enjoyment of luxuries)	*Dainyam* (Humiliation)	*Dharmalabhah* (gain of religious merit)	*Vaimansyam* (enmity)	*Vairi, sukham* (enemies; happiness)	*Bhayam* and *shokashcha* (fear and sorrow)
11.	*Vittapraptih* and *sukham* (gain of money and happiness)	*Vividhartha-labhah* (gain of various types)	*Labhah* and *sukhapraptih* (gain and enjoyment of pleasures)	*Shubham arthagamah* (gain of auspiciousness and money)	*Saukhyam-praptih* (happiness and gain)	*Dukham; dhanagamah* (difficulties; gain of money)	*Sukhavittalabhah* (gain of happiness and money)	*Sukham* and *vittapraptih* (happiness and attainment of money)	*Suyasho-rthalabhah* (good reputation, an gain of money)
12.	*Dravyanashah* and *pidabhayam* (loss of money and danger of pain)	*Rogh; dhana nashah* (disease; destruction of money)	*Rogah; shokashcha* (disease; sorrow)	*Shokah; dhananashah* (sorrow; loss of money)	*Dehe pidabhayam* (danger of physical pain)	*Dhanagamah* (good monetary income)	*Klesham* and *anarthashcha* (grief and heavy loss)	*Hanih* and *pidacha* (monetary loss and suffering)	*Pida* and *vairancha* (suffering and enmity)

Appendix 4

METHOD OF PYRAMIDS FOR OBTAINING AN ANSWER TO A QUESTION

A system of pyramids can be used for getting an answer to a query. For example, let us consider the query: will my partnership with Ramesh be profitable? In this case the method of pyramids may be found useful when a person does not want to use astrological device for finding out whether the *rashis* according to the names indicate beneficial relationship or otherwise.

In forming a pyramid on the basis of a question, one should not apply the value attached to each letter of the alphabets but simply add up the number of letters:

The rules of pyramid formation are as follows:

1. First of all, write down the total number of the words used.
2. Next, write down the total number of letters in each word, keeping in mind that the total should not be more than 9. For example, 13 should be written as 4, and 10 as 1.

3. Finally, the addition of the total number of letters should be written in the form of numbers ranging from 1 to 9 only. The results of the pyramid method should be understood on the basis of the following pattern:

1 – denotes complete success.
2 – denotes uncertainty and obstacles
3 – denotes success after initial obstacles.
4 – denotes excessive obstacles.
5 – denotes complete success as a result of a journey.
6 – denotes favourable period and the cooperation of friends.
7 – denotes obstacles at present but success in future.
8 – denotes doubtful success and intensity of opposition.
9 – denotes elimination of obstacles and of enemies in the near future.

Therefore, developing the pyramid, the following points should be mentioned:

Rules:
1. Add the number of words of a question. For example, there may be eight words in a question.
2. Add the letter of each word used and put this total by the side of the total of the words.
3. In the line below, put first the total of the 1st and 2nd figures, and then the total of the 2nd and 3rd figures, and then the total of the 3rd and 4th figures, and so on till the last figure. The result will be that if there are nine figures in the first line, in the next line we shall have eight and in the line below seven, and so on. This will continue till we have only one figure or number.
4. The total should always be put within the range of 1st to 9. For example, if the addition of 7 and 6 is 13, this will be put as four (1+3 is equal to 4), if the total of 6

and four is ten, it will be put as 1 (1+0 is equal to 1).

Let as consider specific examples to illustrate the aforementioned points.

Example:1.

Will Rakesh's matter be settled within two days?

(4)   (7)   (6)   (2)   (7)   (6)   (3)   (4)

```
8 4 7 6 2 7 6 3 4
  3 2 4 8 9 4 9 7
    5 6 3 8 4 4 7
      2 9 2 3 8 2
        2 2 5 2 1
          4 7 7 3
            2 5 1
              7 6
                4
```

Example 2:

Shall I marry the girl I want? (Total no. of words:7)

```
7 5 1 5 3 4 1 4
  3 6 6 8 7 5 5
    9 3 5 6 3 1
      3 8 2 9 4
        2 1 2 4
          3 3 6
            6 9
              6
```

Example 3:

Will my wife deliver a son this time? (Total no. of words: 8)

```
8 4 2 4 7 1 3 4 4
  3 6 6 2 8 4 7 8
    9 3 8 1 3 2 6
      3 2 9 4 5 8
        5 2 4 9 4
          7 6 4 4
            4 1 8
              5 9
                5
```

Appendix 5

COMMON *GRAHAS* AND *RASHIS* AND THEIR ENGLISH EXAMPLES

Grahas (Planets)

Sanskrit	In English
Ravi or Surya	The Sun
Chandra	The Moon
Mangala	Mars
Budha	Mercury
Guru or Brihaspati	Jupiter
Shukra	Venus
Shani	Saturn
Rahu	Dragon's head
Ketu	Dragon's tail

Rashis (Signs of the Zodiac)

In Sanskrit	In English
Mesha	Aries
Vrishabha	Taurus
Mithuna	Gemini
Karka	Cancer
Simha	Leo
Kanya	Virgo
Tula	Libra
Vrishchika	Scorpio
Dhanu	Sagittarius
Makara	Capricorn
Kumbha	Aquarius
Meena	Pisces